POLITICAL SKILL
AT WORK

POLITICAL SKILL AT WORK

Impact on Work Effectiveness

GERALD R. FERRIS

SHERRY L. DAVIDSON

PAMELA L. PERREWÉ

DAVIES-BLACK PUBLISHING
MOUNTAIN VIEW, CALIFORNIA

First reprinted by Davies-Black, an imprint of Nicholas Brealey Publishing, in 2010:

20 Park Plaza, Suite 610
Boston, MA 02116, USA
Tel: 617-523-3801
Fax: 617-523-3708

3-5 Spafield Street, Clerkenwell
London, EC1R 4QB, UK
Tel: +44-(0)-207-239-0360
Fax: +44-(0)-207-239-0370

www.nicholasbrealey.com

Special discounts on bulk quantities of Davies-Black books are available to corporations, professional associations, and other organizations. For details, contact us at 888-273-2539.

17 16 15 14   10 11 12 13 14 15
Printed in the United States of America

The Library of Congress has previously cataloged this edition as follows:

Ferris, Gerald R.
    Political skill at work : impact on work effectiveness / Gerald R. Ferris, Sherry L. Davidson, Pamela L. Perrewé.—1st ed.
        p. cm.
    Includes bibliographical references and index.
    ISBN 0-89106-210-6 (hardcover)
    1. Office politics.
    2. Organizational behavior. I. Davidson, Sherry L. II. Perrewé, Pamela L. III. Title.
HF5386.5.F465 2005
650.1'3—dc22

                                                          2005016330

FIRST EDITION
First printing 2005

To our parents, children, and grandchildren

CONTENTS

PREFACE

M ost people earn their living in large or small organizations—businesses, nonprofits, educational institutions, or local, state, or national government departments. In group efforts like these, you often need the ability to influence others. Indeed, even the self-employed must deal with customers and other individuals in ways that require influence. But how do you influence others? Force people to comply with your wishes or interests? Threaten them? Intimidate them? No, of course not. You need to develop a style of interaction that allows you to read situations, interpret them, and exhibit just the right kind of behavior to induce others to do what you want—and do it willingly, as if it were their idea. That is, you need *political skill.*

This book is about the nature of political skill and the roles it plays in your ability to influence others, and therefore, in your personal job and career success. It is a how-to as well as a what-to book. That is, beyond describing what to do, it also shows how to do it in ways that will be effective and result in successful influence. Bookstores are full of books of recipes for "winning at office politics"—but their readers do not turn into overnight successes (or even long-term successes) because it takes more than simply knowing what to do; you have to do it in convincing ways and understand the "how" of influence. To know both what approach to take and how to implement it when you need to influence others at work is the essence of political skill.

Not Mere Manipulation

Everyone marvels at those people who are so incredibly good at getting what they want in the workplace: the politicians and high-profile corporate executives who play their constituencies, boards of directors, or shareholders like virtuoso musicians as they pursue their personal agendas. These people have amazing political skill. But political skill is not just something for celebrities. Nor is it simply something you can use to get out of trouble or to get away with self-serving efforts to increase your personal wealth at the expense of many others. Indeed, despite the many and well-publicized instances in the news, this kind of slippery behavior is a misuse of political skill, not an intrinsic part of it. Political skill is an effective and essential characteristic; properly applied, it makes good things happen both for those who use it and for the organizations in which they work.

At one time or another, everyone needs to be able to influence others to follow their ideas, decisions, and new programs of action, and in today's world that takes political skill. So this book is about learning to understand, realize, enhance, and use political skill at work. Indeed, the double entendre in the title is quite intentional: we are interested in political skill at work (in the workplace), but we are also interested in characterizing political skill at work (in the way it operates and how it results in personal and organizational effectiveness).

Structure of the Book

Part One introduces you to political skill, shows you where the interest in political skill came from, and explains why you need it to thrive and survive in organizations today. Also, this section of the book shows how to measure political skill, providing an eighteen-item inventory that allows you to assess your level of political skill. It also discusses ways to train or develop political skill in people.

Part Two shows how you can use political skill for self-improvement and to increase work effectiveness. The chapters in this section address getting hired, maximizing job performance and career success, enhancing your reputation, and coping with stress and facilitating health and well-being. It then discusses how political skill can help organizations realize greater effectiveness through leadership and team performance, and concludes with a brief summary of the book's observations.

The Appendix presents some of the detailed findings from our research into the role of political skill and its relationship to other factors that influence performance in the workplace. In addition, throughout the book, you will see references to scholarly work in this field. The study of political skill has benefited from much careful work that sorts out common knowledge from commonly accepted myth, and the results provide useful background that will allow you to proceed with confidence.

To be an effective leader, you need to possess a number of important characteristics. However, what really distinguishes the best leaders from all the rest is their political skill.

So we invite you to sit back, relax, and let us share with you what we have learned about political skill. Political skill is a fascinating concept, a tool that can help you excel at work; in the pages that follow, we describe just what political skill can do for you.

Acknowledgments

We have been researching organizational politics for more than two decades—over half of that time on the concept of political skill itself—and we have not been working alone. Many colleagues have worked with us over the years and helped us refine our understanding. We would especially like to acknowledge Bill Anthony, Howard Berkson, Randy Blass, Robin Brouer, Mike Buckley, Ceasar Douglas, Don Fedor, Dwight Frink, Dave Gilmore, Angela Hall, Mike Harvey, Wayne Hochwarter, Micki Kacmar, Chuck Kacmar, David Kaplan, Tom King, Bob Kolodinsky, Darren Tread-way, Erin Vickory, Sandy Wayne, Alan Witt, and Kelly Zellars.

Although we have worked hard at defining, studying, and developing a better understanding of political skill, we were not the ones who coined the term. In the early 1980s, Jeffrey Pfeffer and Henry Mintzberg independently wrote about the importance of political skill in navigating the turbulent waters of organizations. We make note of their fine work quite liberally throughout this book, and we wish to thank them for their contributions to our thinking and research over the years.

Writing this book was a quite an experience—at times frustrating and at times exhilarating, but always interesting. And it was a family affair: Ferris and Davidson are brother and sister, and Ferris and Perrewé are husband and wife. Our many phone conversations and trips between Tallahassee and New York all added to the enjoyment.

We would like to acknowledge some good friends and colleagues who helped us during the writing of this book. Ferris and Perrewé want to express their appreciation to Phil Amsellem and Wade Nettles, their personal trainers and co-owners of Elite Fitness. Keeping a regular fitness routine of working out at the gym at 5 a.m. several days a week was important to both our mental and physical stamina, and we thank Phil and Wade for keeping us on track.

Ferris had both knee surgery and shoulder surgery during the twelve months this book was being written, which introduced some challenges and difficulties, particularly the four months spent in physical therapy for the shoulder. He would like to extend his appreciation to his physical therapist, Larry Johnson of Tallahassee Orthopedic and Sports Physical Therapy, for his hard work, patience, and support through this tough time.

Certainly, we would be remiss if we did not acknowledge the support and encouragement we received from our publisher, Davies-Black. Special thanks go to our editor, Connie Kallback, whose belief and commitment made this project possible—thanks much, Connie, we express our deepest gratitude. We would also like to thank Laura Simonds, Jill Anderson-Wilson, and the entire staff at Davies-Black Publishing for their professional approach, attention to detail, and interest in quality production.

ABOUT THE AUTHORS

G erald R. Ferris is the Francis Eppes Professor of Management and professor of psychology at Florida State University. Prior to accepting this chaired position, from 1999 to 2000 he held the Robert M. Hearin Chair of Business Administration and was professor of management and acting associate dean for faculty and research in the School of Business Administration at the University of Mississippi; before that, from 1989 to 1999 he served as professor of labor and industrial relations, of business administration, and of psychology at the University of Illinois at Urbana-Champaign and from 1991 to 1996 as director of the Center for Human Resource Management at the University of Illinois.

Ferris received a Ph.D. degree in business administration from the University of Illinois at Urbana-Champaign. He has research interests in the areas of interpersonal and political influence in organizations, performance evaluation, strategic human resources management, and the components of reputation as they affect behavior in organizations. He is the author of more than 125 articles published in such scholarly journals as the *Journal of Applied Psychology, Organizational Behavior and Human Decision Processes, Personnel Psychology, Academy of Management Journal,* and *Academy of Management Review,* and such applied journals as the

Academy of Management Executive, Human Resource Management, Human Resource Planning, and *Organizational Dynamics.* He served as editor of the annual series *Research in Personnel and Human Resources Management* from its origin in 1981 until 2003. He has also authored or edited a number of books including *Human Resources Management: Perspectives, Context, Functions, and Outcomes* (Prentice-Hall), *Handbook of Human Resource Management* (Blackwell), *Strategy and Human Resources Management* (South-Western), and *Method & Analysis in Organizational Research* (Reston).

Ferris has consulted on a variety of human resources topics with companies including ARCO, Borg-Warner, Eli Lilly, Motorola, and PPG, and he has taught in management development programs and lectured in Austria, Greece, Hong Kong, Japan, Singapore, and Taiwan, in addition to various U.S. universities. His studies of influence at work have been the focus of considerable general interest as well, and he has been interviewed on *CBS This Morning* (by Charles Osgood) and on radio stations for call-in programs in most major U.S. cities, as well as on the BBC in London and stations in Tokyo, Singapore, and New Zealand. His work has been written up in major U.S. newspapers from coast to coast.

Sherry L. Davidson is an early childhood consultant and researcher at New York University's Child and Family Policy Center. She received her master's degree in special education and a Ph.D. degree in educational administration from New York University's Steinhardt School of Education. Currently, she is working with a team of professionals on a federally funded project to improve the quality of New York City's early childhood programs. In addition to her prior experiences as a classroom teacher in both regular and special education, she has worked as a manager in the private business sector. Her research, teaching, and managerial experience have provided her with a distinctive and varied appreciation for the dynamics of influence and politics in organizational settings.

Pamela L. Perrewé is the Distinguished Research Professor and Jim Moran Professor of Management in the College of Business at Florida State University. She received her bachelor's degree in psychology from Purdue University and her master's and Ph.D. degrees in management from the University of Nebraska–Lincoln. She primarily teaches courses in organizational behavior and human resource management; she has taught at the undergraduate, master's, and Ph.D. levels. She is a past recipient of the Florida State University Teaching Excellence Program award and the University Teaching Incentive Program award as well as the University Developing Scholar award. Her research interests focus on the areas of job stress, coping, organizational politics, emotion, and personality.

Perrewé has published more than ten book chapters and seventy articles in journals such as *Academy of Management Journal, Journal of Management, Journal of Applied Psychology, Journal of Organizational Behavior, Journal of Vocational Behavior, Human Relations,* and *Journal of Applied Social Psychology,* and she has presented seventy-five research papers at academic and professional meetings. She serves on the editorial review board for *Journal of Occupational Health Psychology, Human Resource Management Review, Organizational Analysis, Leadership and Organizational Studies,* and *Journal of Managerial Issues.*

She has Fellow status in the Southern Management Association, the Society for Industrial and Organizational Psychology (SIOP), and the American Psychological Association (APA). Further, she was recently invited by then U.S. Secretary of Health and Human Services Tommy Thompson to serve a three-year term on the prestigious Board of Scientific Counselors of the National Institute for Occupational Safety and Health (NIOSH), in conjunction with the National Centers for Disease Control and Prevention. She is coeditor of an annual research series titled *Research in Occupational Stress and Well-Being,* published by Elsevier.

PART I

UNDERSTANDING POLITICAL SKILL

CONSIDERING THE NATURE
OF POLITICAL SKILL

Political skill has a bad rep, conjuring up images of behind-the-scenes manipulation, self-interested behavior, and favoritism at its very worst. Of course, people have used their skills to mask their abuse of position and authority, but that's not what political skill *is*. We present a more balanced perspective here, outlining the skill set necessary to operate effectively and create an environment where trust and relationship building are the norm. Real political skill is a positive force, and it is essential for job and career success in organizations today.

To thrive in today's workplace, you need to understand what to do and how to do it in genuine, sincere, and convincing ways. You also need to know when and how to put yourself in the proper place and stance on an issue to take advantage of and even create opportunities. The interesting thing about political skill is that if you have it, you appear not to have it—as Dale Dauten writes in the *Chicago Tribune*, the way you can tell a master of political skill is "You can't. That's their genius" (1996, p. 2). Truly skillful execution is usually perceived as genuine, authentic, straightforward behavior.

Being able to influence others at work through persuasion, orchestrating support, and inspiring trust and confidence is the essence of political skill. In this chapter we discuss how and why such skill is absolutely critical to success and effectiveness at work and then lay out the basic elements of the skill.

Importance of Social Effectiveness in Organizations

In the past couple of decades, conditions have changed almost out of recognition for organizations of all types. Globalization, downsizing, restructuring and redesign, mergers and acquisitions, and telecommunications have changed the ways organizations look and function so dramatically that the business schools need new theories to explain how things work in this new world (Daft & Lewin, 1993).

Classic organizational theory was built on the concept of bureaucracy and the policies, systems, and features that went along with it. The traditional bureaucracy is a stack of layers; it has a formalized chain of command and division of labor based on information flowing up and orders flowing down. Recent changes and new work structures have increased unstructured interaction among work team members, peers as well as supervisors and subordinates, and directly between employees and clients. It is less and less possible to be considered good at your job if you're not also good at working with and influencing others. A brief tour of the new organizational theory will illustrate the importance of political behavior in the social mechanism.

Redefining Jobs and Qualifications

In essence, the current organizational changes are forcing redefinition of the term *job* itself. Rather than carrying out the fixed, static duties and responsibilities of the past, today's employees find themselves coping with the dynamic, fluid, and constantly changing sets of roles needed to adapt to turbulent contexts (Cascio,

1995). Work is organized at the group or team level, where people interact collaboratively and interdependently to produce products and services. The knowledge, skills, and abilities required to be effective in these settings are increasingly social and political— you still have to know the job itself (engineering, mechanics, computer programming, biology, whatever—matters researchers group under the label *simple domain expertise*), but that kind of knowledge is no longer sufficient.

More and more organizations are reacting to these changes in the nature of work by trying to staff jobs on the basis of *fit:* an assessment of how well the prospective recruit matches the qualities and characteristics of the team or group and the organization's overall culture. Tasks and duties of a particular position can be used as its reference point, but beliefs, values, and personal qualities must be perceived as meshing with team, group, and organizational culture or the applicant loses out. More important from the point of view of our argument here, the decision is made very rapidly—and that means that simply possessing the requisite qualities does not guarantee success when you're applying for a job; you must present the proper face, and that requires political skill.

Reexamining Work

Traditionally, "doing your job" meant carrying out the specific technical tasks and duties in your formal job description, which spelled out the key outcomes you were responsible for. In recent years, however, the phrase has expanded to cover a variety of interpersonal, social, and motivational aspects of performance that are neither formally designated nor required, but that are nonetheless valued by the organization.

Contemporary thinking on job performance now regards it as having two categories: *task performance,* the traditional elements of a job description, and *contextual performance,* the elements inherent in all jobs that support the social fabric of the organization

(Borman & Motowidlo, 1993). When it comes to this second category of performance, a main component is *interpersonal effectiveness*, or the extent to which you can maintain good relations with supervisors, co-workers, and others in the organization (Murphy & Cleveland, 1995). Contextual performance also includes volunteering, helping, cooperating, following rules, persisting, and so forth.

As Walter Borman and his associates (2003) point out, both research and practice have shown that these types of behaviors influence supervisor evaluations of employee performance, arguably through the social effectiveness with which such contextual performance behaviors are carried out. Borman makes the additional assertion that the two types of performance can be predicted from different measures: task performance by measures of intelligence or cognitive ability and contextual performance by measures of social effectiveness and personality. From our work, however, we have come to believe that this complex array of measures is unnecessary, as political skill is a strong predictor of both task and contextual aspects of job performance.

What Is Political Skill?

Organizations are political arenas. Almost everywhere you look, informal negotiation and bargaining, deal making, exchanges of favors, and coalition and alliance building characterize the way things really get done. That is easy to see, but it is much harder to define the characteristics that enable one person to succeed in this unstructured environment while another fails. Some have referred to such qualities as interpersonal style, savvy, street smarts, and political skill. However, to date few researchers have tried to move beyond anecdote and innuendo to develop a more precise notion of political skill: what its components are and how you might know it when you see it—and thus be able to measure it, practice it, and develop it in yourself and others.

Although job performance, effectiveness, and career success do depend in part on intelligence and hard work, other factors

such as social astuteness, positioning, and savvy also play important roles. When the term *political skill* was first introduced in the
literature—by Jeffrey Pfeffer (1981) and Henry Mintzberg (1983),
working independently—it was identified as a competency that
was needed for success, and one that involved the exercise of influence through persuasion, manipulation, and negotiation.

But we can trace the origin of the concept of political skill
back further. Its historical roots are grounded in the interestingly
similar but separate writings of psychologist E. L. Thorndike and
entrepreneur Dale Carnegie, both working in New York in the
early 1900s. Thorndike (1920) introduced the concept of *social
intelligence,* which referred to understanding people and acting on
that knowledge in influential ways. Carnegie (1936), through his
still-famous courses on interpersonal effectiveness, taught fundamental principles of how to work with and through others. This
scientific and applied work formed the foundation for the importance of social and interpersonal competence in organizations,
and specifically, for political skill.)

Definition

We define political skill as the ability to understand others at work
and to use that knowledge to influence others to act in ways that
enhance one's personal or organizational objectives. That is, politically skilled individuals combine social astuteness with the capacity to adjust their behavior to different and changing situational
demands in a manner that appears sincere, inspires support and
trust, and thus influences the responses of others.

Politically skilled individuals exude a sense of personal security
and calm self-confidence that attracts others and gives them a
feeling of comfort. This self-confidence never goes so far as to
come across as arrogance; it is always displayed at the proper level
to be seen as a positive attribute. Therefore, although self-confident,
those high in political skill are not self-absorbed—their focus is
outward toward others, not inward and self-centered. This allows

politically skilled individuals to maintain proper balance and perspective and also ensures they keep a healthy gauge on their accountability to both others and themselves. Indeed, this is similar to Rosabeth Moss Kanter's (2004) discussion of her "confidence" concept, when she suggests that confidence is properly balanced so it is neither arrogance nor conceit, which make you lose perspective and become complacent.

We suggest that people high in political skill not only know precisely what to do in different social situations at work but how to do it in a manner that disguises any ulterior, self-serving motives and appears to be sincere. Note that we are not asserting that the politically skillful necessarily *have* ulterior, self-serving motives, only that their behavior will be the same regardless of their underlying motives. Political skill is a tool. Without it, you can be absolutely sincere and devoted to the common good and still find that people doubt your motives and withdraw from you.

Furthermore, we see political skill as independent from intelligence or cognitive ability, because it is a different sort of competency and does not depend for its effectiveness on mental acuity. The two can certainly occur together, but it is entirely possible to be highly politically skilled without possessing an unusually high IQ. Someone can possess modest or even below-average intelligence and still be very politically skilled. Likewise, it is possible to possess very high intelligence and disastrously low levels of political skill—the nerd and the dork are icons of popular culture for good reason. In terms of its development, we believe that some aspects of political skill are dispositional or inherited, but others can be developed or shaped through a combination of formal and informal training and experience (see Chapter 3).

Facets of Political Skill

Careful examination of interaction on the job, with particular reference to what we know about political skill (even if not explicitly referred to by that term), indicates several important factors:

social astuteness, interpersonal influence, networking ability, and apparent sincerity. Social astuteness (the ability to read and understand people) and interpersonal influence (the ability to act on that knowledge to get what you want) come first, but the ability to build connections, friendships, networks, alliances, and coalitions is also critical for navigating the politics of organizations.

Many scholars of organizational life have emphasized these points. For example, Jeffrey Pfeffer writes, "Having connections, having allies, is important for developing and exercising influence" (1992, p. 175). And Fred Luthans put it this way: "[Networking is] a system of interconnected or cooperating individuals. It is closely associated with the dynamics of power and the use of social and political skills" (Luthans, Hodgetts, & Rosenkrantz, 1988, pp. 119–120). Luthans also noted that activities associated with networking were, by far, the ones that received the most time and attention from successful managers.

The most essential aspect of political skill is genuineness or sincerity. It is not just what you do but how you do it—carrying out each influence attempt in ways that appear sincere and genuine, without ulterior motive—that inspires trust and confidence.

In Dale Carnegie's best-selling book *How to Win Friends and Influence People,* his first rule of how to make people like you was to become genuinely interested in them. Carnegie's point has been much discussed and promoted over the years, and it can be reduced to Richard Stengel's cogent advice: "Never find fault, never argue, flatter people at every opportunity, appear sincere" (2000, p. 203). Carnegie argued that liking was a precursor to effective influence, and many influence researchers since his time have agreed that this is critical to successful influence.

Political skill has four critical facets:

- Social astuteness

- Interpersonal influence

- Networking ability

- Apparent sincerity

Social Astuteness
Individuals possessing political skill are astute observers, keenly attuned to diverse social situations. They comprehend social interactions and in social settings they accurately interpret their own behavior as well as that of others. They have strong powers of discernment and high self-awareness. This characteristic has been referred to as "sensitivity to others," and as Pfeffer suggests, "Somewhat ironically, it is this capacity to identify with others that is actually critical in obtaining things for oneself" (1992, p. 173). Socially astute individuals often are seen as ingenious in dealing with others.

Interpersonal Influence
Politically skilled individuals have a subtle and convincing personal style that exerts a powerful influence on those around them. Individuals high in interpersonal influence nonetheless are capable of great flexibility, appropriately adapting and calibrating their behavior to each situation so as to elicit particular responses from others.

An important feature of flexibility that contributes to success at interpersonal influence involves "focusing on ultimate objectives and being able to remain emotionally detached from the situation" (Pfeffer, 1992, p. 176). Those high in interpersonal influence appear to others as being pleasant and productive to associate with, and they use such behaviors to control their environments. Although these individuals are not always overtly political, they are seen as competent leaders who play the political game fairly and effortlessly. This graceful political style is seen as a positive rather than negative force within the organization.

Networking Ability
Individuals with strong political skill are good at developing and using diverse networks of people. People in these networks tend to

hold assets the organizer sees as valuable and necessary for personal and organizational success. Politically skilled individuals easily develop friendships and build strong, beneficial alliances and coalitions. Furthermore, individuals high in networking ability carefully position themselves to both create and take advantage of opportunities (Pfeffer, 1992). Masters of the quid pro quo, they are often highly skilled negotiators and dealmakers, and they are adept at conflict management. Described in these terms, their activities may sound cold and manipulative, but they are nonetheless essential; as Watkins and Bazerman point out, "Executives need to build good networks—both informal advice networks and formal coalitions—for influencing political decisions" (2003, p. 80).

Politically skilled individuals enjoy the respect and generally also the liking of those in their network, resulting in significant and tangible benefits, such as gaining favorable reactions to ideas, enhanced access to important information, and increased cooperation and trust. They know when to call on others for favors, and they are perceived as willing to reciprocate. In addition, they inspire commitment and personal obligation from those around them. In short, politically skilled people possess high levels of social capital, which enhances their reputation and ability to be influential.

Apparent Sincerity

Politically skilled individuals display high levels of integrity, authenticity, sincerity, and genuineness. They are (or at any rate appear to be) honest, open, and forthright. This dimension of political skill strikes at the very heart of whether influence attempts will be successful, because it focuses on the perceived intentions of the behavior in question. And perceived intentions or motives are what shape the whole response: for example, your offer to stay and help out after work is labeled "citizenship" if your boss thinks you really care about the goal of the effort, and "political" if your boss figures you expect to get something out of it. (This conclusion is both common sense and supported by research; Bolino, 1999.)

Influence attempts will be successful only to the extent to which the actor is perceived as possessing no ulterior motive.

Because their actions are not interpreted as manipulative or coercive, individuals high in apparent sincerity inspire trust and confidence. Their tactics often are seen as subtle, but their motives do not appear self-serving. They are capable of disguising ulterior motives when necessary, yet others would not describe them as hypocritical. Instead, they appear to others as being exactly what they claim to be. In *Leadership* (2002), Rudolph W. Giuliani portrays himself as a straight shooter with an aggressive style that can be characterized as "what you see is what you get." The leadership he displayed on and around the events of September 11, 2001, earned him the title of not only "America's Mayor" but also "Mayor of the World" (Purnick, 2004, p. 1). Giuliani is an example of someone who is politically skilled and appears to others to be sincere and genuine. Whether he is truly sincere and genuine is not the point—it is entirely possible to be sincere and genuine and still be perceived as sneaky and self-serving, and vice versa. Regardless of the underlying reality, you need political skill to inspire trust and confidence in others.

How Political Skill Differs from Other Concepts

Researchers find it useful to assess concepts such as political skill to determine the degree to which they resemble other concepts in related fields. We present such a discussion here and, in more depth, in the Appendix. If your own interest in the topic is more focused on what you can do with it, you may prefer to look ahead to the following section.

In our view, political skill is related somewhat (but not too strongly) to selected personality traits and to other constructs that purport to measure social effectiveness or interpersonal sensitivity, such as self-monitoring, agreeableness, and conscientiousness. However, we would expect these relationships to be only modest in size.

At its core, political skill reflects the capacity to exercise effective influence over others at work. Therefore, it should be related to particular types of influence tactics such as exchange, upward appeal, and coalition building, but less to assertiveness. The exchange tactic reflects favors given in return for favors. Upward appeal tactics involve obtaining the support of individuals higher up in the organization, whereas coalition tactics refer to lining up co-worker or subordinate support, building strength in numbers. Assertiveness involves demanding, ordering, setting deadlines, and checking up on others in order to exercise influence. We suggest that when those high in political skill engage in influence tactics, they do so in an effective way.

Furthermore, we believe that political skill generates an increased sense of self-confidence and personal security because such individuals should experience a greater degree of control over activities at work. Indeed, such greater self-confidence and control should lead individuals high in political skill to experience significantly less stress or anxiety at work. Consequently, political skill may serve as an antidote of sorts to the negative consequences of stress.

Emotional intelligence has received considerable attention in the popular, business, and research press in the past decade, primarily as a function of Daniel Goleman's (1995, 1998) best-selling books. Emotional intelligence focuses predominantly on the emotion-based aspects of interpersonal effectiveness, influence, and control. Conversely, we see political skill as incorporating knowledge and skill that go beyond emotions. Therefore, we propose that emotional intelligence correlates positively with political skill, but not so highly as to suggest complete overlap or redundant constructs.

Some might argue that competencies like political skill are simply a function of intelligence, with more intelligent people possessing more of such competencies. As noted earlier, we disagree with that view, and instead suggest that political skill is not related at all to intelligence or cognitive ability.

Finally, we differentiate political skill from social skill, although on the surface the two concepts may appear very similar. Social skill generally refers to competencies in communication and the ease, comfort, and connectedness with which individuals interact with others. Political skill as we define it goes beyond mere ease and facility of interaction; it focuses on managing interactions with others in influential ways that lead to individual and organizational goal accomplishment.

Political Skill and the Influence Process

In the large and growing body of research into organizational politics, few studies include attempts to evaluate the political skill of the influencer, leaving readers uninformed about why influence efforts succeed or fail. Indeed, most work to date has assumed that the mere demonstration of an influence attempt is the same as its effectiveness. However, it is not enough to study what people do—the particular influence tactics or political behaviors they attempt to use—without attending to the context. Political skill is what determines both the selection of influence tactics to use in a particular situation and the successful execution of those tactics.

Political skill operates in a number of ways to affect, and ensure the success of, the influence process in organizations. Individuals high in political skill know which particular type of influence tactic or strategy to employ in each situation, but that, in itself, is not enough. Skilled individuals also know precisely how to execute each selected tactic or strategy in just the right way to obtain the desired effect and thus ensure the success of the influence attempt. For example, consider just two commonly used influence tactics: ingratiation and self-promotion. Each of these tactics can be perceived and interpreted (by those you are trying to influence) quite differently based on whether you display high or low political skill in your choice and execution.

Ingratiation

Ingratiation refers to behaviors that are designed to get you "in good" with others and be liked by them, either as an end in itself or as a way to gain access to some rewards or benefits. The effort is sometimes regarded as simple flattery, but we like Richard Stengel's definition: "strategic praise, praise with a purpose" (2000). Stengel adds, "It may be inflated or exaggerated or it may be accurate and truthful, but it is praise that seeks some result, whether it be increased liking or an office with a window. It is a kind of manipulation of reality that uses the enhancement of another for our own self-advantage. It can even be genuine praise" (pp. 14–15).

Because ingratiation is a strategic effort to gain or achieve some outcome, the individual employing it needs to be concerned with how it is perceived, which largely is a function of how effectively it is presented. Essentially, ingratiation is an attempt to influence others that absolutely must appear to be sincere if it is to work at all—even though it is often quite insincere. Political skill is what distinguishes successful ingratiation from the crash-and-burn failures that are dismissed as attempts to suck up to the recipient. That is, the very same behaviors and statements can be interpreted as either positive ("What a nice person") or negative ("What a manipulative attempt to influence me").

Also, even when an ingratiator can disguise any ulterior motive from the target of influence and thereby hook the target, bystanders (for example, co-workers or others observing the influencer in action) tend to find it much easier to see the ingratiation for what it really is. For example, think back to the 1960s television series *Leave It to Beaver*, and remember Eddie Haskell's thinly veiled attempts to butter up June Cleaver—and the eye-rolling reactions of Beaver, Wally, and Ward Cleaver, who did not get sucked into his efforts but saw them for what they were. (Actually, June Cleaver did too, because Eddie's political skill level was so incredibly low!) Eddie Haskell is the classic low-political-skill person who has such poorly developed self-awareness that he doesn't realize how he comes across to others. Consequently, he is perceived as insincere, as an apple-polisher, a suck-up, or a brown-noser (whatever your preferred term), which leads people not to like him.

Self-Promotion

Self-promotion has the objective of projecting competence, and involves trying to show how effective you are, what good things you've done, and so forth. Obviously, self-promotion can be a bit tricky to pull off well in modern Western culture, which requires people to walk a fine line when talking up their skills and achievements. Too little emphasis, and you appear to understate things and fail to impress people; too much emphasis, and you appear arrogant, conceited, and self-important. Once again, the difference in how self-promotion comes across depends on your political skill. People with low political skill are seen as schmoozers and braggarts who are saying and doing whatever they can just to get ahead. Ironically, people high in political skill are perceived as not being politically skilled at all—they are viewed as genuine, sincere, authentic, and what-you-see-is-what-you-get.

Interestingly, the climate on self-promotion seems to be loosening up somewhat. Whereas bragging about oneself in the workplace used to be regarded as quite inappropriate and not an effective way to get ahead, some are beginning to argue that bragging is a good thing, essential to get you noticed and evaluated favorably. Peggy Klaus, in the aptly titled *Brag! The Art of Tooting Your Own Horn Without Blowing It* (2003), maintains that bragging is an absolute necessity in the workplace today. To refuse to brag and insist on remaining quiet often means no one appreciates all you do, and you may even find others taking credit for your accomplishments. Donald Trump has been characterized as an excellent self-promoter, and it is difficult to argue with his success.

Political Skill in Action

What does seem apparent in all the discussions about ingratiation and self-promotion or bragging is that their success mostly depends on the style of delivery—the way you execute this kind of influence behavior. It is the politically skillful who manage to pull these efforts off well enough to be perceived as favorable: honest praise, confident but humble acknowledgment of genuine personal strength. Without political skill, ingratiation and self-promotion efforts will be interpreted as hypocrisy, arrogance, and conceit—characteristics everyone finds negative.

Political skill obviously plays a key role in the dynamics of both ingratiation and self-promotion as they are demonstrated and interpreted in the workplace. However, ingratiation and self-promotion represent just two tactics of influence available, which suggests a key point about political skill we made earlier: you have to do the right thing at the right time in the right way.

That is, politically skilled individuals will astutely assess every situation to determine the most appropriate methods and techniques of influence to employ in that context and then execute them to perfection. People high in political skill will not simply master one or two tactics and proceed to apply them across the board, because some tactics are not appropriate for certain situations and are thus bound to fail there no matter how well they are executed. Instead, politically skilled individuals create a diverse portfolio of tactics they can employ selectively—and individually or in combination—to create strategies of influence.

People Low and High in Political Skill

To put the definition of political skill in context, it is useful to look at some examples. Interestingly, individuals seen as having ulterior motives probably are not very good at influence attempts. They are low in real political skill even though they may see themselves as political operators. It is the individuals who come across as genuine, sincere, and authentic in their statements and behavior—and who do not appear to be trying to influence people at all—who are actually high in political skill. It is also possible to have good and noble intentions but still be unable to inspire comfort and trust because of a lack of political skill.

AL GORE AND BILL CLINTON

Former U.S. vice president Al Gore, who is very bright, comes off as wooden or fake, illustrating the point that political skill is not simply intelligence but something very different. As we've said, a person can be high in one and low in the other, and Gore is a vivid example. He is probably an honest, caring individual who really wants to be influential in positive ways and to inspire people to trust and follow his ideas. Unfortunately, in running for president, he just didn't come across the way he wanted to. He never achieved Bill Clinton's genuine, sincere image in public interactions, which remained virtually undimmed despite the troubles surrounding the latter part of the Clinton presidency.

The American public wants desperately to trust and feel comfortable with its leaders, and to perceive them as authentic and as the real thing. However, Howard Gardner noted, "even the claim for authenticity can be manufactured (good actors know how to feign sincerity), while many 'authentic' individuals simply look awkward or amateurish when sitting under klieg lights" (1995, p. 60).

THE CHARACTERS IN *BROADCAST NEWS*

The fate of people with high and low political skill has also been featured on stage and in movies. One of the best examples of this is the 1987 hit *Broadcast News*. In this movie, Tom Grunick (played by William Hurt) is an attractive and politically skilled news anchor who cannot write and lacks the intelligence to understand the news he is reporting. As a news anchor, Tom is much loved—he is engaging, seemingly genuine, and authentic in his news delivery. In spite of his low IQ, he is successful because of his political skill. Meanwhile, Aaron Altman (played by Albert Brooks) is extremely bright, well read, and motivated. He has everything it takes to be a successful news anchor, except political skill. Aaron has no clue how to relate to others and does not understand why it is important to do so. He simply wants to report the facts—and he is good at getting them. Unfortunately, because of his lack of political skill (he is arrogant and boring, lacks charisma, and is not appealing to the audience), Aaron is kept back in the newsroom.

Clearly, having both intelligence and political skill is valuable. However, for many positions, political skill is more likely to lead to success than IQ.

Conclusion

Possessing the qualities of political skill is more essential for job success today than ever before. Because of the importance placed on political skill, working professionals should be interested in their own level of political skill, essentially asking themselves, How politically skilled am I? The next chapter answers this question with a tool that measures political skill using the four dimensions examined in this chapter: social astuteness, interpersonal influence, networking ability, and apparent sincerity.

MEASURING POLITICAL SKILL

No matter how high you've climbed or how good you are already, it makes sense to enhance your political skill. As we define it, political skill can help literally everyone in an organization improve their success at work whether they primarily interact with one person at a time or in a large team or group setting. If you make decisions about hiring, promotion, and retention, you need the political skill to make those decisions smoothly and to recognize the skill levels of the people you choose to bring in and keep. Likewise, if you contract for outside services in marketing or lead a customer services team—or lead or serve on a team of any sort—political skill is an important competency for you.

But how can you tell if you have it? To determine how much political skill you have and what dimensions need development, you need a systematic means for measuring it. This chapter presents just that—our own measurement tool, an easy-to-take inventory that is useful to anyone in any group or any type of organization.

Taking the *Political Skill Inventory*

The *Political Skill Inventory* (PSI) is an eighteen-item questionnaire that will give you a score indicating your general level of political skill. Overall political skill is the combination of social astuteness, interpersonal influence, networking ability, and apparent sincerity. You'll recognize these as the four dimensions introduced in Chapter 1, and the PSI can also measure each of these.

Now take a moment to complete the PSI. The important thing to remember is that you must be honest with yourself when completing this survey. It is easy but pointless to game the system here; if you concentrate on getting a high result for the overall assessment or any of the dimensions, the exercise will be useless to you—neither you nor anyone else will know how well you did. Play it straight and answer honestly, and you will get a true reading that will help you understand what dimensions you need to work on.

Rating Your Political Skill

If you have completed the PSI and calculated your overall political skill score, you should have a number between 1 and 7. We consider a score of 4 to be the midpoint of political skill, so if you have a total score of 4, you have average political skill. If you scored lower than 4, you have less than average political skill; if you scored higher than 4, you have greater than average political skill. In general, a score of 1 or 2 is considered low; 3, 4, or 5 is considered average; and 6 or 7 is considered high.

Successful managers normally score fairly high on the PSI. Remember, political skill has four separate dimensions, and each dimension involves two different issues: First, do you have the ability, and second, are you motivated to use it? Based on previous research (e.g., Semadar, 2004), the following sections examine the four different aspects of political skill and provide some development strategies to help you increase each one.

Political Skill Inventory

Instructions: *Using the following 7-point scale, write in each gray circle the number that best describes how much you agree with that statement.*

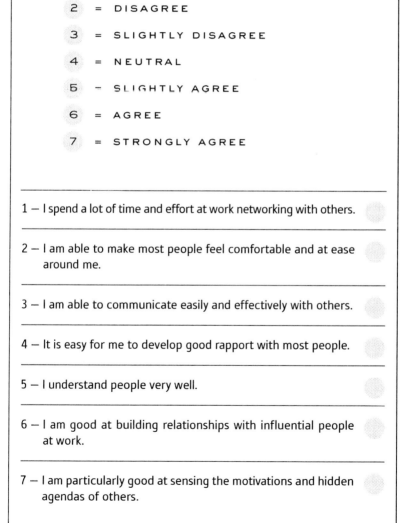

1	=	STRONGLY DISAGREE
2	=	DISAGREE
3	=	SLIGHTLY DISAGREE
4	=	NEUTRAL
5	=	SLIGHTLY AGREE
6	=	AGREE
7	=	STRONGLY AGREE

1 — I spend a lot of time and effort at work networking with others.

2 — I am able to make most people feel comfortable and at ease around me.

3 — I am able to communicate easily and effectively with others.

4 — It is easy for me to develop good rapport with most people.

5 — I understand people very well.

6 — I am good at building relationships with influential people at work.

7 — I am particularly good at sensing the motivations and hidden agendas of others.

8 — When communicating with others, I try to be genuine in what I say and do.

9 — I have developed a large network of colleagues and associates at work who I can call on for support when I really need to get things done.

10 — At work, I know a lot of important people and am well connected.

11 — I spend a lot of time at work developing connections with others.

12 — I am good at getting people to like me.

13 — It is important that people believe I am sincere in what I say and do.

14 — I try to show a genuine interest in other people.

15 — I am good at using my connections and network to make things happen at work.

16 — I have good intuition and am savvy about how to present myself to others.

17 — I always seem to instinctively know the right things to say or do to influence others.

18 — I pay close attention to people's facial expressions.

TOTAL =

÷ 18 = ◯

SCORING

Compute your overall score by adding together your response scores on all the questions and dividing the total by 18. You will have an overall political skill score between 1 and 7. Larger scores identify people who have higher political skill, and smaller scores identify people who have lower political skill.

MEASURING THE
FOUR DIMENSIONS OF POLITICAL SKILL

You can also compute your score for each of the four dimensions of political skill—social astuteness, interpersonal influence, networking ability, and apparent sincerity—by adding up the responses to the questions that measure each dimension and then dividing by the number of questions.

Dimension of Political Skill			
Social Astuteness	Interpersonal Influence	Networking Ability	Apparent Sincerity
5 ___	2 ___	1 ___	8 ___
7 ___	3 ___	6 ___	13 ___
16 ___	4 ___	9 ___	14 ___
17 ___	12 ___	10 ___	
18 ___		11 ___	
		15 ___	
Total =	Total =	Total =	Total =
÷ 5 = ◯	÷ 4 = ◯	÷ 6 = ◯	÷ 3 = ◯

Social Astuteness

Questions 5, 7, 16, 17 and 18 on the PSI measure social astuteness.

What your score means. A low score on the social astuteness dimension of the PSI means you likely have a low level of understanding of the motivations or intentions of others' behaviors, or a low desire to understand them, or both. A low score also means you have little intuition or savvy about how to present yourself to others and you do not always know the right things to say or do in order to influence others.

An average score means you have a satisfactory ability to understand people and a reasonable ability to read people's motivations and to detect any hidden agendas they may have. An average score represents a satisfactory level of intuition and savvy about how you come across to others and also means you often know the right things to say and do in order to influence others.

A high score means you have an excellent ability to understand people, sense their motivation, and detect any hidden agendas. You have outstanding intuition and the savvy to know how to present yourself. Also, when influencing others, you seem to instinctively know exactly the right things to say and do.

Development strategies. If you would like to improve on your social astuteness, remember that in order to understand others, you must listen. This in part means not interrupting others while they are speaking. Try to repeat what the other person has said by paraphrasing so you are clear that you know what that person is trying to convey. By trying to really listen to what someone is saying, you not only help yourself understand it better, you communicate to the speaker that the message is important to you! Show respect for others' ways of thinking and they will be likelier to respect yours.

Interpersonal Influence

Questions 2, 3, 4, and 12 on the PSI indicate interpersonal influence.

What your score means. A low score on the interpersonal influence dimension means that you have a fairly low ability or motivation to make people feel comfortable and at ease with you. You may not have a smooth communication style with others at work, and you probably have a limited ability to develop a good relationship and rapport with most people.

An average score means you have a satisfactory level of ability to make people comfortable and at ease around you. You are normally able to communicate with others, but not always or with everyone. You also have a reasonable ability to establish a good rapport with most people.

A high score means your ability to make people feel at ease around you is strong. You probably have an effective communication style with others and are able to establish a good rapport with most everyone you meet. Most people are quickly drawn to you because you know how to make yourself likable.

Development strategies. Influencing others often means finding a way to give them something so that you can achieve your goal. Do not simply ask for things without considering others' situation. Think about what other people might need in exchange for carrying out your wishes. Make sure you understand how your request might affect them negatively and think about a possible trade. For example, if you would like someone to work late for you, perhaps you could allow some time off later in the month. Appeal to the common good for both of you.

Networking Ability

Questions 1, 6, 9, 10, 11, and 15 on the PSI measure networking ability.

What your score means. A low score on the networking ability dimension means you either have a low ability to develop relationships with others at work or you lack the motivation to spend time and effort developing these relationships, or both. A low score also means you probably lack a large support network that can be used to advance your work goals.

An average score means you have a satisfactory ability and motivation to spend time and energy developing work relationships with others. An average score also means you probably have a reasonable formal and informal network of people that can help you move work-related goals forward.

A high score means you are an excellent networker. You have both the ability and the motivation to develop positive work relationships. You are especially good at developing good relationships with influential people. You probably have many support networks, both formal and informal, that you often use effectively to move your goals forward in the organization.

Development strategies. Those who are skilled at networking are also those who share useful work information. This is not gossip but information that will help people do their jobs better or information that will help them gain a better perspective about the department or company. Further, they remember important things about the people with whom they work.

A general rule of thumb is to have three pieces of information you remember about everyone; this can be knowledge about something at work, educational background, or even something personal.

Skilled networkers are approachable. Sometimes you will need to initiate the relationship; initiating a contact can be done as simply as asking someone a question. If you want to improve your networking skills, do not wait for others to come to you!

Apparent Sincerity

Questions 8, 13, and 14 on the PSI measure apparent sincerity.

What your score means. A low score on the apparent sincerity dimension means you have a limited awareness of the importance of appearing genuine and sincere. Also, you probably show a relatively low level of interest in other people and do not place a high value on being perceived as genuine and sincere.

An average score means you have a satisfactory level of awareness regarding the importance of appearing genuine and sincere. You probably show some interest in some of the people with whom you work. You also place a reasonable value on being perceived to be genuine and sincere.

A high score means you have a good appreciation for the importance of appearing genuine and sincere to everyone. You aspire to demonstrate a sincere interest in others at all times. It is also important for you to be perceived as being genuine and sincere.

Development strategies. Being sincere comes from having a kind and caring frame of mind. One way to demonstrate sincerity is by listening carefully to others. Unfortunately, many managers are poor or only marginal listeners. They have an action orientation and are likely to interrupt by cutting someone off in midsentence. Some are impatient and even try to finish other people's sentences for them. This impatience and unwillingness to listen carefully to others is often interpreted as insensitivity, which may translate into a perceived lack of caring. Thus one way to increase your apparent sincerity is simply to listen to others.

Appearing to be genuine and sincere also depends on your nonverbal communication. Keep eye contact with the person talking. Looking past the person to see who else is around or looking at your watch to catch the time can be translated as not being sincere and not caring about the person with whom you are talking.

Appearing genuine and sincere is a lot easier when you like the person or when you are talking with someone who could have a strong effect on you, like the CEO of your organization. However, it is important for your political skill to appear sincere to those you do not like. Remember to nod when another person is talking; this lets the person know you are listening and makes you seem more engaged in the conversation.

Improving Your Overall Political Skill

People who are high in political skill are able to work from the outside situation inward. They are able to determine the demands in their surroundings and the requirements of each situation. They are able to talk with someone and quickly know the right tone and style of communication to use to best influence them. To improve your overall political skill, practice viewing your surroundings, then reaching inward for your response to them. What are some ways to accomplish this?

First, if you want others to agree with a particular proposal or idea, it is usually a good idea to informally discuss your proposal with influential others prior to presenting it in a public forum. Trying to get informal agreement with or approval of (particularly from those who often raise objections) your proposal will help to ensure your idea will go forward.

Second, organizations are political by nature. People with political skill have the savvy to foresee and understand the trappings and dead ends within the organization. They know how to get things done quickly and by whom. They also know the gatekeepers—the people who have control of important information and resources. Look around and figure out how your organization works.

Third, be sensitive to others. Those high in political skill are able to read others and predict how they will react to various approaches. Learn how to read nonverbal communication so you stay connected with someone. Signs like a slouched stance, crossed arms, and repeated glances at a watch or clock indicate that it's probably time to ask a question to get your listener back into the conversation. If this does not work, do not continue to bore ahead. Realize that it is time to cut off the conversation.

Finally, try to keep any conflicts to a minimum. The more conflict, the less control you have over the situation. Separate the person from the topic or problem; try to avoid blaming someone for a problem. The best strategy is to attack the problem, not the person presenting it.

Asking Others to Rate Your Political Skill

Self-report measurements of political skill can be useful and enlightening, but it's not easy to give the true answers instead of the right ones. The temptation is strong to answer the questions in a socially desirable way whether or not those answers reflect the real scores—and, indeed, the person completing the questionnaire may not be aware of the real scores. It's all too easy to wind up in the position of Eddie Haskell on *Leave It to Beaver*, proceeding with self-confidence while others snicker at your efforts.

These difficulties make it a good idea to consider collecting political skill data from a variety of sources. A work group can prepare the PSI for one another, for example, engaging a trusted outsider to assemble average ratings for each member so they can see where they stand without being distracted by knowing the opinions of specific associates. It can also be used as a form of 360-degree rating, going beyond the job incumbent to ask the subject's immediate supervisor, peers or co-workers, and perhaps even direct reports if there are any. As organizational researchers, we've found that approach useful in verifying the measure's ability to tap meaningful elements of interpersonal effectiveness by demonstrating that it generates some consistent level of employee political skill agreement from superiors, peers, and subordinates.

Conclusion

The *Political Skill Inventory* can help people at any level in an organization measure the general level of political skill they possess. It can also measure their ability in each of the four dimensions of political skill: social astuteness, interpersonal influence, networking ability, and apparent sincerity. Throughout the book, we examine further these four dimensions and the roles they play in hiring, job performance, reputation, job stress, and leadership and team performance.

Now that you know your political skill scores and what they mean, we will turn to methods that can help you develop your political skill. The next chapter focuses on different ways to teach (and learn) political skill.

3

DEVELOPING POLITICAL SKILL

Politically skilled individuals are astute in understanding social situations, influential in getting others to follow their lead, adept at networking and building social credit (often called *social capital*), and at least apparently genuine and sincere in their interpersonal interactions. We view political skill as a competency that is at least in part inborn but is also one you can shape.

Robert Jackall provides a quick checklist of the characteristics of an effective organizational politician (1988, pp. 46–47). Can you answer yes to the following questions?

- Am I able to engage in the appropriate behavior in different situations?

- Do I have the ability to read and conform to social situations?

- Can I control my emotions and my expressions of emotion to convey a proper image?

We argue that it is political skill that differentiates truly effective managers from ineffective managers.

As we noted in Chapter 1, we view political skill as an interpersonal style, one that combines social astuteness with the capacity to adjust to different and changing situational demands in a manner that inspires trust and confidence, conveys sincerity, and influences others to respond favorably. It is this characterization of political skill that guides our efforts to train and develop such competencies in the people we work with.

Although the capacity for political skill is to some extent inborn, it must be trained—and it can be trained to some extent even without a strong natural propensity for it. What it boils down to is that no matter how great your natural aptitude, if you never work on political skill or are never put in situations that bring it out and develop it, it will not be realized. If you have any capacity for political skill—and that capacity is far more widespread than many people realize—we believe that there is much you can acquire through careful shaping and development. Precisely how this shaping and developing take place is the focus of this chapter.

Shaping and Developing Political Skill

Most of today's formal education conveys content-related knowledge while ignoring the skills of human interaction and effective influence. For example, business schools do a great job on the basics of accounting, finance, marketing, and management, but most fail to teach the importance of political skill for career success. Even corporate training programs that attempt to focus on developing interpersonal skills often fall short—in part because the learning environment does not feel safe. Participants see such skills as gateways to promotion or advancement, and that makes it hard to take risks ; who wants to make mistakes while others are watching (and probably evaluating)? If political skill training is to be effective, participants must be put in a noncompetitive and supportive environment where to be fair, everyone in the room joins in all the activities.

Furthermore, such classroom learning as occurs is very difficult to transfer into the work environment. Many organizations have concluded that they're wasting their time and resources on classroom training, particularly in soft skills areas such as interpersonal communications and negotiation. We believe that by its very nature, political skill defies conventional training and education. Therefore, traditional lecture-oriented training methods can play no more than a secondary role to more active, experiential, and involvement-related techniques.

In this book, we focus on the behaviors and competencies that make up the four dimensions of political skill. The training and development methods we present are those that work to build and develop the dimensions of political skill severally and together. We single out drama-based training and executive coaching for special attention because these techniques are particularly useful for all four dimensions and for the population in general. We then discuss specific methods for each dimension, and wind up with a section devoted to issues that mainly affect the development of political skill among women and minorities in the business environment.

Drama-Based Training

Nearly two decades ago, the *New York Times* reported on a then-new form of training for managers and executives that involved taking acting classes (Drake, 1987). Now, with hundreds of companies employing it to instruct and train employees and managers, this drama-based alternative has become a successful industry. More than ever, today's training must be compelling, realistic, practical, relevant, and lasting. The training should also encourage risk taking and facilitate improved awareness and behavioral flexibility. Drama-based training does that by providing an opportunity to step outside real-world roles and personalities, making it a useful vehicle to shape and develop functioning political skill. Participants actually learn (rather than merely hear about) emotional regulation and control, recognition and response to nonverbal cues, management of tone of voice, and so forth.

Dramaturgical approaches possess a degree of power and practicality inaccessible to classroom training. They embed the trainees in realistic roles that simulate the day-to-day social interactions encountered at work. Depending on the sponsor's goals, different levels of drama-based training will be suitable. (For more on this point, see St. George, Schwager, & Canavan, 2000.) For example, if increased awareness about a particular work-related issue (say, sexual harassment or unethical work practices) is the goal, low-impact drama-based training can be used to reach large audiences relatively quickly. In general, low-impact training involves reading or listening to scripted scenes or vignettes that focus on the chosen work-related issue. In an organizational training workshop on sexual harassment, short stories or vignettes that describe different types of sexual harassment and give examples of incidents involving each type might be read to participants.

As with low-impact training, moderate-impact drama-based training helps increase awareness, but it adds audience participation (such as calling for questions or breaking up for small-group work) designed to explore the thoughts, emotions, and motivations of each audience member pertaining to the training content.

High-impact training abandons the actors or readers entirely. Instead trainers work out scenarios with the training participants themselves. To help people gain new skills they will be able to use on an ongoing basis, high-impact drama-based training must be highly customized, targeted, improvisational, context-focused, and flexible. Trainees thus become actively involved in the training content, which brings its impact home in ways no secondhand presentation can achieve.

High-impact drama-based training is particularly effective for developing political skill. Like the other drama forms, it is especially effective in increasing awareness that aids social astuteness. Unlike other drama forms, it involves interaction among the participants in real work issues and in their equivalent occupational capacities. Training content also can be targeted to develop specific political skill dimensions. Here's a sample vignette:

> The trainee takes on the role of a worker trying to influence a peer to work late one evening. The peer (played by an experienced trainer) does not want to work late, but would do so if a satisfactory quid pro quo were extended. Rather than saying this straight out, the peer will give the sort of subtle cues (saying things like "I was thinking about going to a ballgame..." or "Tonight's not the best night for me to work late...") that people use in real life to indicate persuadability and will then wait for the trainee to make such an offer.
>
> At any stage during the drama, the action can be frozen, the trainee asked about current thought processes, alternatives considered, and emotions felt. By asking questions that encourage deeper thinking and alternative ways of behaving, as opposed to giving answers, the trainer can allow the drama to continue until it looks like the trainee has expanded in formerly unconsidered ways. The influence transaction more easily transpires once the trainees realize that they have to give something to get something—and do so in a genuine way. Similar vignettes can be scripted to focus on improving genuineness or sincerity (for example, dealing with a co-worker's loss of a close family member) or building networks (for example, developing a high-powered team for an ad hoc project that requires after-hours work).

In such scenarios, trainees learn at a gut level that the way they speak is as important as the words they say, if not more so. They come to understand (as opposed to simply know) that a repertoire of influence tactics paired with target situations is not enough for effective influence. Drama is particularly good for training participants' capacity to differentiate and apply a variety of delivery styles in ways that build political skill.

Executive Coaching

As you move up the hierarchy to jobs with broader scope, technical expertise declines in importance and political skill increases. In fact, when the Center for Creative Leadership (CCL) studied why once-promising executives failed on the job—what the researchers called "executive derailment"—lack of social effectiveness emerged as a leading cause (Lombardo & McCauley, 1988). Success at the upper levels is largely determined by possession of sufficient political savvy to obtain scarce resources and muster support.

The CCL derailment studies outlined ten fatal flaws that led to failure, and more than half dealt with issues such as insensitivity to others, perceived arrogance, failure to delegate, excessive ambition, inability to adapt to a boss, and overdependence on someone. Only one of the ten flaws had anything to do with making the business work. Political savvy and interpersonal issues appear to be far more difficult than technical issues for many people to master on their own. When they find themselves in positions that require political skill, those fortunate enough to recognize the problem are increasingly often calling on executive coaches for assistance.

The executive coaching process usually begins with an assessment by the coach. Using the assessment as a guide, the coach and the executive jointly determine what issues the executive is dealing with. At this point, a strategy can be formulated concerning types of changes that need to be made and skills that need developing. In line with the CCL results, the change and development process generally focuses on the areas we term political skill.

Executive coaching is an ongoing process that depends heavily on the relationship between the two parties. No one has found any quick fixes when developing the kind of behavior that coaching is designed to facilitate. We believe that it is a good idea to set up a coaching contract that runs at least a year and that anything less than six months may do more harm than good.

Executive coaches help the executive identify issues likely to affect performance in the executive role. The coach also works with the executive to develop new behaviors and provides ongoing feedback to develop the subtle changes in behavior that can enhance the executive's effectiveness. After considering various alternatives and evaluating likely consequences, the executive can choose a way to approach this situation, and perhaps role-play the strategies with videotaped feedback. Such role-playing exercises are immensely useful even though they cannot, of course, ensure that the real target of the strategy will react like the partner in the scenario, because the rehearsal and feedback encourage the executive to think through the situation and prepare for obstacles.

For example, financial services provider Wachovia Corporation offers an extensive coaching program to a broad spectrum of executives. People in the top levels of the company use external coaches to help them face challenges that without question require political skill, like moving into a new position or dealing with a merger. At lower levels, internal coaches from different divisions within the company partner with university professors to provide 360-degree feedback and action plans to managers.

Executive coaching increases psychological and social awareness and understanding, increases tolerance for ambiguity and range of emotional responses, and increases ability to develop and maintain flexibility in effective interpersonal relationships, all of which are central to political skill. A skilled coach can help you become more conscious of politically charged environments and more astute at observing political situations and people. Over time and with practice, you can refine novice skills into a well-integrated skill inventory and smooth style that will help you deal effectively with a wide array of situations.

Methods for Developing Social Astuteness

To develop social astuteness, people need feedback about their social interactions, including the level of awareness and understanding they display and the various alternatives open to them for response. In addition to drama-based training and coaching, a number of other training and development methods can enhance self-awareness and social astuteness. Two we have found most useful are critique and feedback sessions and videotaped role-playing with feedback.

Critique and Feedback Sessions

Critique and feedback sessions can range from 360-degree feedback and evaluations to one-to-one discussions. If such interactions are positive, constructive, and developmental—as opposed to negative and personal—they can do a lot to help people understand their strengths and weaknesses as well as identify specific areas for improvement. These sessions can significantly increase awareness of, for example, behaviors that are seen as either too assertive or too submissive for certain situations. As a result, the sessions themselves become a source of valuable data to both the providers and receivers of the feedback. A great deal of real-world learning regarding how to deal with others can take place in such sessions, which are often rich in emotionally charged content for all participants. In addition, participants who already possess political skill can use their abilities to model appropriate behaviors for other participants.

Videotaped Role-Playing with Feedback

Another method for developing social awareness and helping people learn more astute ways of interacting with others is to videotape role-playing sessions. This approach works best when the participants are all members of the organization (as opposed to trained coaches) who have an assortment of levels of social astuteness. As we noted in the discussion of drama-based training, role-playing some of their jobs' challenging interpersonal dilemmas helps people gain a better understanding of the skills required to be effective. Videotaping the sessions and playing them back for class critique makes these skills even more apparent. The intent of the role-play is to teach problem-solving and interpersonal skills and to support the participants in developing real resolutions to problems. An important by-product of such role-playing sessions is that individuals become more aware of their social behavior and also of various responses from those with whom they are interacting. Pausing the videotape and offering feedback at critical junctures allows participants to evaluate other alternatives that they can draw on in the future.

Developing Interpersonal Influence

Perhaps more here than for the other three dimensions, the use of many different kinds of training will make it easier for you to develop the skills to persuade and ultimately control the behavior of others. The more avenues you explore, the more you will enhance your comprehension of each situation and the variety of responses open to you. Critique and feedback sessions and videotaped role-playing with feedback are effective for this component as well in the context of social astuteness. Other techniques we find particularly valuable for increasing influence skills include leadership training, behavioral modeling, mentoring, and developmental simulations.

Leadership Training

Leadership training experiences, sometimes called human relations training, have been prevalent since the 1950s. Such programs typically involve such activities as case analysis, role-playing, problem solving, and communication exercises. Effective leaders need skills in communication, empathy, goal setting, coaching, and other issues related to influencing others. Helping managers develop into leaders is a primary focus of such programs, in which learning how to influence others is a primary goal. Ultimately, the most effective leaders have followers who willingly and enthusiastically work to help achieve the vision, goals, and priorities set by the leader.

Behavioral Modeling

Based on Albert Bandura's (1986) social learning theory and often incorporated as part of overall leadership training, behavioral modeling is perhaps the primary interpersonal skills training technique used in business today. Experts typically use the role-play format to model particular skills, after which the participants practice the skills repeatedly so as to internalize them and make them usable on the job. We suggest that the best way to practice influencing others is to use the new skills in any social setting in which the occasion for influence arises. These settings may or may not be in a work capacity.

In combination with drama-based training, behavioral modeling supports powerful political skill development programs. The following example illustrates how these techniques can be combined to develop influence skills:

The trainers begin by spelling out the definition of political skill to the trainees, with particular emphasis on the four dimensions. Then the trainers (or actors brought in for the purpose) act out a vignette concerning how a common on-the-job problem is handled poorly (with little or no political skill) and then handled effectively (with high political skill). For example, a vignette might feature a performance review meeting where a subordinate who is perceived to have excellent potential but has yet to live up to it faces a supervisor with low political skill, who focuses solely on the poor performance and insists that such performance will not be tolerated for much longer.

After a round of discussion, the trainers repeat the scenario, this time role-playing the behavior of a supervisor with high political skill who begins by asking the subordinate's views on the subordinate's own performance. After hearing the subordinate's views, the supervisor will respond accordingly, demonstrating various facets of the four dimensions of political skill as appropriate.

If the subordinate appears to be devastated and apologizes for the poor performance, for example, the trainer can model good political skill by offering feedback on the comments (demonstrating good listening skills) and telling the subordinate not to go overboard. Knowing that the subordinate is devastated already, the supervisor can choose to use a gentler approach (coaching rather than reprimand) in working to improve performance.

The vignette can play out in many ways, and it may well be worth showing the trainees more than one—the subordinate falsely claims to be overworked, is really overworked, has personal problems that make work inordinately difficult, and so on—and the politically adept response in each case. (It's probably not a good idea to present too many variations on the ham-handed retort, however. Most employees have seen plenty of that already.)

Besides advising specific action in the role-plays, supervisors might offer a potential mentor from their social network to help subordinates work on areas that need strengthening. Throughout each role-play, trainees are encouraged to take notes and ask questions. After the role-playing, a thorough program matches trainees with one another to practice the new skills with real issues facing them in their organizations.

Mentoring

Another effective way to develop influence skills is to assign individuals to work with skilled mentors. Individuals can observe professionals in real-work situations as they exercise influence in meetings with subordinates and peers. The mentors use language, facial expressions, body posture, and gestures to convey messages to observers as to how influence is best exercised. The keys are to be sure that individuals are assigned to talented and understanding mentors who have plenty of social influence interactions and the individuals are given plenty of opportunities to discuss the interactions encountered. Hence, effective mentors not only model effective influence behaviors, so that protégés learn by observation, they also take time to discuss various social interactions so that protégés can completely understand how and why mentors behaved in such a manner.

Organizational mentoring relationships focus primarily on building political skill in protégés and helping them develop a richer and more informed understanding of the work environment. Such relationships do a great deal to promote personal learning, because good mentors increase learning that relates to both job skills and interpersonal competencies—including political skill.

Protégés are apprentices who are shown the practices of the business world and are educated in the political ways of the game within the organization. The political skill developed by the protégés actually may be the most critical set of skills that they acquire in their entire careers. The information passed to protégés provides the necessary road map for the boundaries and the informal rules of the game.

At its best, mentoring involves the informal training and development of what, when, and with whom to do things in the work environment, along with building the perceptive, interpersonal, and social effectiveness competencies that round out political skill.

Developmental Simulations

Simulations of work-related situations where participants must exercise influence can be very effective as a learning experience, especially if followed by a discussion and critique by peers. For example, picture a smart but disagreeable computer programmer who combines truly superior work with a sour attitude that makes everyone else's work harder. By playing such a part with verve, a trainer could help participants in the program stretch their minds to come up with new and better influence tactics and strategies to try.

Developing and Managing Networks and Social Capital

Social networks are both a sign of effective political skill and an essential part of its exercise. You must know the right people—the people who can help you meet your goals and objectives—to be confident of acquiring resources, gaining access, and otherwise exercising influence. Successful networking requires more than knowing how to build connections, allegiances, and contacts; you also have to understand how to use social capital to develop coalitions when support needs to be mobilized. More than simply exchanging favors, building a network also involves skills in inspiring people to support and follow you.

Some of the techniques we've covered for other political skill dimensions will also help people learn to build and maintain a social network. Drama-based training and critique and feedback sessions, for example, can be extremely useful in providing pertinent feedback to trainees about ways to develop social capital. Vignettes or feedback sessions can be focused entirely on how various individuals developed (or failed to develop) relationships with people holding valued resources. Session participants who know each other in a work-related context can be particularly helpful in recommending alternative ways to build valued networks.

Leadership training and behavioral modeling are both particularly helpful in encouraging individuals to take risks and try new behaviors in social contexts. For example, trainers or skilled actors can model effective ways of negotiating with others that provide for synergistic, win-win outcomes that lead to future dealings with valued partners.

Ideally, protégés can gain the confidence they need to build networks by spending time with a mentor. Politically skilled mentors will already possess valued networks and can explain the various ways in which their networks were built. Protégés can then apply the mentors' strategies to build their own networks. In some cases, the mentor's network can directly benefit the protégé, who effectively becomes a part of it.

Team-Based Training

Team training activities are especially useful in giving individuals practice in developing a network. Such activities work best if they last at least a few days and if they involve valued outcomes that require networking to mobilize complementary human resources.

Counseling

For individuals who are meek or frightened about taking risks to expand their social contacts, we recommend counseling with a professional skilled in helping clients improve social relations. Counseling is valuable not only for the timid but for overassertive individuals as well. For those who come on too strong, whose extroversion eventually wears out its welcome with others, counseling can probe for causes of such behavior and encourage greater restraint.

Building Credit

Any networking education program needs to emphasize the importance of being—and therefore being seen as—a valuable partner. Participants must remember that they become part of the network of anyone who enters their network, so whatever they do that makes others view them as effective gives them a sort of credit balance that they can draw against when they need support for their aims. Commonsense ideas for building social capital include volunteering, being generous with favors, doing high-quality work, getting the job done on time, and getting others excited about working with you. Effective networkers form allegiances and coalitions with other effective people by demonstrating their understanding and ability to help with the job. They are scrupulous about honoring their commitments, promises, and allegiances.

Additionally, effective networkers never lose track of the point that networks can go on for a long time. Lack of any current need for a particular person's assistance does not mean that it may not be vital in the future. Never burn your bridges with anyone. Every contact you maintain will help develop a resource-rich network that will ultimately aid you in your various work and nonwork endeavors.

Developing Genuineness or Sincerity

In many respects, apparent sincerity is the real core of what makes political skill work, because it involves being able to exert influence in a manner that does not appear or feel like an influence attempt. The fundamental error people make is overdoing it, coming on too strong, and thus being perceived as manipulative— all of which makes their influence targets question their motives and react negatively.

Effective communication skills that are inspirational and influential are certainly part of the development and shaping of political skill. When Annette Towler and Robert Dipboye (2001) investigated the nature of charismatic communication training, they found that people receiving such training employed more animated gestures, more analogies and stories, and were perceived by others as more effective communicators than those receiving only presentation training. Communication training is also useful because it emphasizes empathy and attention to non-verbal cues and tone of voice.

Many people instinctively reject the idea of training in charismatic communication, feeling that deliberate efforts along those lines must be deceptive and two-faced—acting one way but believing another. In practice, however, it is rare for anyone to be able to present even the most genuine beliefs convincingly without knowing how to convey the desired impression. We maintain that political skill itself is a neutral force that need not and should not be employed with manipulative or deceitful intent. We are not suggesting training in misrepresenting the truth or in how to be dishonest without appearing to be so. To inspire trust and confidence for the long term, we believe that the most effective influence attempts are made in a truthful, empathic, genuine manner—and that doing so is a skill that can be learned and practiced like any other.

Drama-based training and behavioral modeling techniques are probably best for demonstrating, for example, alternative ways of showing sincerity or insincerity. Actors could role-play various levels of sincerity for different situations along a continuum from insincere, cold, and blunt to sincere, warm, and gentle. Expressing condolence for a death in the family of a co-worker requires different body language and concern than congratulating someone on winning the lottery. Such genuineness variations could be modeled by trainers (or actors) and then practiced by trainees.

Deceivers and Believers

For purposes of simplicity, we propose that there are essentially two types of characters who reflect high political skill and use it to influence others. Furthermore, we suggest that the prognosis for the long-term effectiveness of influence efforts is different for each type.

The two types of characters are "Deceivers" and "Believers," and they differ not so much in their observable short-term or immediate behavior but rather in the believability or perceived sincerity of their interpersonal influence behavior over time. Deceivers are concerned with the immediate accomplishment of the influence objective. They concentrate on playing a role convincingly enough to elicit the desired response from the target or object of influence. This would be synonymous with "surface acting" in the dramaturgical literature, and therefore, even if Deceivers can be effective in the short term, it is unlikely they can continue to play the role convincingly with others, day in and day out.

Believers fully embrace and internalize the persona they demonstrate when influencing others. They are not merely playing a role, even one that has been well scripted. They literally become the person they intend to represent in the interpersonal influence attempt. This would be synonymous with "deep acting," and it is likely that Believers will be effective in successfully demonstrating influence behavior in a sincere way both immediately and over the long term because they are just being themselves.

Drama-based training helps participants learn to see the differences between Deceivers and Believers, a distinction that also can be seen among professional actors themselves.

DENZEL WASHINGTON IN *REMEMBER THE TITANS*

Denzel Washington is well known and widely respected for how he practices his craft and the depth within which he immerses himself in some of the movie roles he takes on—for example, in *Remember the Titans*, a fact-based account of a newly integrated Virginia high school in 1971 and of Herman Boone, the hard-nosed African American coach who led the team to the Virginia state high school football championship. As usual, Washington (playing Boone) turned in a superb performance, but there seemed to be something special about this performance that differentiated it from his other great roles.

When asked about his portrayal of the crusty football coach and how he played the role so convincingly, Washington commented that he met with Herman Boone, and he researched the role to better understand the racial climate in 1971 in that part of the country—essentially, preparing the way he normally would for a movie. However, he then mentioned that once filming started, he was either on the set filming his part, or he completely isolated himself in his trailer, which allowed him to delve deeper and deeper into the Herman Boone character. He suggests that if he played a convincing part, it was because he was not playing the role of Herman Boone, he had actually become Herman Boone, and was just playing himself.

Insights from an Acting Coach

We interviewed New York actor and acting coach Mara Hobel to gain greater insight into the art of acting. She contended that in order to appear authentic, an actor must not only understand the role but also "capture the essence of that character." Hobel explained that techniques such as tone of voice, voice inflection, and facial expression contribute to a genuine stage presence that is "absolutely essential for a believable performance." She indicated that an actor must use all dimensions of his or her being to engage the audience. Hobel added, "It is most captivating when the actor suppresses emotion. The audience reads the body language on a subconscious level, like pantomime." Therefore, self-control is a major factor in making a true emotional connection.

In her role as an acting coach, Hobel communicates to her students that, on stage and in life, actors "need to take responsibility for 'who' and 'how' they are influencing others." Hobel told us, "I tell my students my shortcomings. I'm honest. They need to know I'm human. When I speak to people I'm not acting, I'm being myself." Thus self-awareness, sensitivity, and being confident in who you are contribute to an authentic presence off- and onstage. As veteran stage actor Lewis Stedden aptly stated, "You can't be a phony onstage."

All this translates to political skill in the workplace. To be a Believer rather than a Deceiver takes a great deal of political skill—a matter not only of words but of tone and inflection of voice, silences, gestures, facial expression, and pauses combined—coupled with deep feeling for the purposes you present.

Political Skill Deficiency of Women and Minorities

It would be nice to be able to proclaim that sex discrimination and race discrimination in organizations are things of the past and that there is true equality for all. However, the reality is that women and ethnic or racial minorities are not faring nearly as well in the workplace as white males are. Many explanations for this disparity have been proposed and debated over the years. One explanation, which directly implicates a lack of political skill, is most useful and interesting for our purposes here.

According to organizational research, women consistently rank higher than men on performance measures ("As leaders, women rule," 2000). Why, then, aren't more of them controlling and running large corporations? Although thousands of very talented women graduate from business schools each year and 45 percent of them work in managerial positions, few women end up as CEOs of major corporations. Why are they not making it to the very top? Research shows that women spend so much time getting their reports perfect and working hard to get great results that they rarely leave their offices to network with others (Isaacson, 2004). We argue that women and minorities will have many more opportunities for advancement if they expand and exercise their political skill.

The Rules of the Game

Political skill itself often represents privileged information that is passed on selectively in organizations to certain newcomers, allowing them to be more successful at work. Mentoring and the informal transmission of information are the principal vehicles by which "the ropes," "the rules of the game," and so forth are passed on. This process also conveys valuable information about alliance building, along with access to influential networks where important behind-the-scenes transactions take place.

This takes on the aura of a private club where only certain individuals are allowed membership, and they typically bear a striking resemblance to those who make up the power elite in organizations—white males. Consequently, women and racial or ethnic minorities must do without such information and therefore must compete for pay, promotions, and other valued organizational rewards against privileged individuals who have been well schooled in the rules of the game and have developed strong political skill. Indeed, women and minorities in such competitions are competing on an uneven playing field in a game in which they do not know the rules.

There seems to be support from many sources for the importance of political skill to success in organizations, and therefore, for political skill deficiency as an explanation for the lack of success of women and minorities.

This observation is far from new. John Fernandez (1981) suggested that a keen understanding of the political aspects of management was perhaps the most important training that women and minorities needed as they approached management positions. Others have argued that political skill was critical to career success for members of diverse groups (Rosen & Lovelace, 1991), and political skill has been identified as a barrier to the advancement of women in organizations (Mann, 1995).

Some progress is being reported on this front, however. A particularly innovative example is MentorNet, an online networking resource that helps women in the fields of engineering, science, and mathematics. More than eighty universities (including MIT and Princeton) and twenty companies (including AT&T and Cisco) match female students with mentors in their fields, providing the students with real-world information and access to networks before the students even join their firms.

Political skill is essential for career success and it becomes more important as one ascends the corporate ladder. When Sallie Krawcheck became CEO at Smith Barney, she inherited the fallout from the Wall Street scandals of the 1990s, including parent company Citigroup's $400 million fine for defrauding investors and a company culture that put its interests ahead of those of its customers. Repairing the damage required political savvy, and Krawcheck began by apologizing—over and over again. She visited thirty-five cities, listening as thousands of clients recounted tales of portfolios demolished by Smith Barney's recommendations on Enron and WorldCom stocks. Winning back trust takes time and political skill, and Krawcheck is using both to restore Smith Barney's damaged reputation.

Women Less Likely to Use Political Skill

Sandi Mann (1995) contends that women tend to have less power than men in organizations and therefore tend to engage in politics less frequently, which puts them at a decided disadvantage. Women are not as likely to use politics and influence to get ahead. Instead, they tend to play by stated or traditional rules and have what amounts to a political skill deficiency. Women tend to view career success as linked with task accomplishment and expertise. They believe that they should and will be rewarded (promoted) in organizations if their work is good enough, and they are competent enough. Many women, therefore, simply do not see the necessity of political maneuvering. This political deficiency relegates them quickly to the losers' bracket and probably explains what appears to be active and blatant gender discrimination in promotion and advancement.

In *Our Separate Ways: Black and White Women and the Struggle for Professional Identity* (2001), Ella Bell and Stella Nkomo point out that many of the women with whom they spoke emphasized the importance of informal networks in career advancement. They observe that in most corporations excellent performance is necessary for advancement but is not the sole criterion. Getting ahead also depends on access to informal networks through mentorships, sponsorships, and help from colleagues. Further, they argue that the more important relationships become, the less important is the actual business at hand, as arbitrary business decisions are made because of relationships. One of the things Bell and Nkomo observe is the continuing strength of the Old Boys' network. Women and minorities don't really break down the wall by advancing upward; they climb over the wall, but the wall, unfortunately, remains intact. Perhaps one way for women and minorities to advance upward and through the wall is through the use of the political skill and networking they gain in mentoring relationships.

Men use informal systems built on the notions of loyalty, favor trading, and protection and view politics as part of the rules of the game. They use informal systems to gain access to early information and to read political currents within the organization. Women, in contrast, tend to rely on the formal organizational system for information and support and view politics as an impediment. As a result of denying the value of corporate politics, women are often politically naive and ignorant. This limits their ability to recognize and build relationships with powerful people within the organization that can give them an advantage in their careers. Through the mentoring process, women should be able to sharpen their political skill, and in so doing, they should be able to operate from a stronger base of networks and social capital and consequently enhance their career progression.

Conclusion

This chapter highlights various ways political skill and its dimensions can be developed. Drama-based training, with its emphasis on involving participants emotionally, is particularly effective in demonstrating various ways political skill can be developed and practiced. Executive coaching is an increasingly popular technique for helping top managers recognize political situations and then learn to develop effective strategies for dealing with them. Other effective methods for understanding and building political skill include critique and feedback sessions, videotaped role-playing with feedback, leadership training, behavioral modeling, mentoring, and developmental simulations.

Political skill is becoming increasingly recognized as a critical competency, essential for job and career success throughout organizations. It therefore needs to be incorporated into the broader repertoire of key competencies to be included in human resource education and development needs for the future.

PART II

USING POLITICAL SKILL FOR WORK EFFECTIVENESS

4

Hiring for Fit

Political skill is not the only thing you need to get a job, but it makes a big difference. After all, most openings draw more than one applicant with the requisite intelligence, education, and experience, so political skill is usually decisive in the selection process.

People high in political skill tend to be more successful at receiving high ratings of suitability for jobs and actual job offers from interviewers—a point supported by research (Higgins, 2000), as well as by common sense. This is most likely because politically skilled people are viewed as fitting the job context better than less politically skilled individuals are, and hiring for *fit* (roughly defined as appropriateness for the mix of personalities, the culture, and the values of the job, the organization, or the work unit or group) has become an increasingly prevalent basis for selection decisions.

In this chapter, we examine the hiring process in organizations today, and how the notion of fit is increasingly being used to decide who gets jobs and who does not. We also describe the role of political skill in assessments of fit and final hiring decisions and provide examples that illustrate the importance of political skill in getting jobs.

The Hiring Process

Most people make their living by working for others, and those others are almost always part of an organization. Would-be employees generally have to clear many hurdles to get hired. Although the official hiring process is sometimes bypassed out of favoritism or personal friendship, most selection systems call for information gathered over a sequence of steps with a final decision being made only after all information is gathered and compared on all job candidates.

Hiring was not always a systematic process. The rise of the factory system during the Industrial Revolution of the late eighteenth and early nineteenth centuries moved the manufacture of goods from individual craftsmen, operating out of their homes and shops, to large numbers of people brought together to work in ways that capitalized on economies of scale and mass production, which increased profitability for business owners. In those days, people typically were hired for jobs that required no prior experience and no special skills. Therefore, hiring was usually first-come, first-served—those who arrived first at the application office went to work.

Psychology in Hiring

In the very early years of the twentieth century, German psychologist Hugo Münsterberg relocated to the United States and settled in Boston. The discipline of psychology was still very new. Münsterberg had received his training in one of the first formal psychology programs in the late 1800s in Leipzig, Germany. Trained in experimental psychology, he believed that the basic principles of psychology could be applied to understanding people's behavior in the workplace (he later became known as the "Father of Applied Psychology").

It just so happened that Boston was experiencing some problems with its transportation system. At that time, the conventional way to get around large cities like New York, Chicago, and Boston was on trolley cars operated by railway motormen. The requirements for holding the job of railway motorman were essentially nonexistent, so people were hired on a near-random, first-come basis. As a result of this hiring process (or lack thereof), Boston was experiencing a costly problem: poor performance, high turnover, and other on-the-job troubles.

Münsterberg approached the city and told them he could help fix the transit system by applying a more systematic and scientific approach to hiring the railway motormen. He first observed and analyzed the job to see what tasks, duties, and behaviors were required, and then he translated that information into the knowledge, skills, and abilities (KSAs) needed to perform these duties effectively. Then he identified the best ways to measure or assess these critical KSAs in job applicants, arguing that the applicants who scored highest on the key KSAs would show the best potential for the job.

Boston implemented Münsterberg's plan, and it worked! Railway motormen hired using this new system consistently performed better, stayed on the job longer, and generally saved the city a lot of money. What Münsterberg came up with was the first formal personnel selection system, which became the standard model for selection and hiring for the next century. (For more on this pivotal event, see Münsterberg, 1913, and Dulebohn, Ferris, & Stodd, 1995.) Further, even this early, Münsterberg understood the critical nature of the human element; he noted that of the three great factors (in the terms of his day, material, machine, and man), man is not the least but the most important. Interestingly, within the past decade or so, more and more companies have been going about the hiring process with that insight in mind, and this approach seems to be driven by the concept of *fit*.

Selection Based on Fit

As university professors, we interact frequently with corporate recruiters who travel to college campuses a couple of times a year to interview students who are completing their undergraduate or graduate degrees. When chatting with the recruiters, we typically ask them what they are looking for in our students—usually for jobs in human resources management—and the exchange that follows has become quite predictable. The recruiters all quickly reply, "I'm looking for someone who fits." We ask just what that means, and the invariable response is "You know, someone who fits." We explain that although we are confident that fit means something specific to them, we don't know what that is, and we ask if they could try to explain it. After some struggle, they inevitably say, "I can't describe it, but I'll know it when I see it."

The Nature of Fit

Herein lies the interesting and sometimes frustratingly elusive issue of fit as a criterion. Some efforts have been made to study the notion of fit and to try to develop a more specific sense of what it means, but the outcome has rarely been of much general help.

It's possible to be a bit more precise about the concept of fit if you can answer the question, Fit for what? In this case, it becomes clear that fit assessments can measure job applicants against different reference points in the organization, including the job, the team or work group they might be joining, the organization's culture, or perhaps even a set of values the organization embraces. The extent to which job applicants are viewed as fitting well with (or being similar to) one or more of the relevant criteria or reference points usually results in their receiving higher ratings of suitability for the job and improving their chances of obtaining job offers.

The Employment Interview and Fit

The employment interview has been—and will doubtless continue to be—the prevalent personnel selection device, the tool employers use to determine how well job applicants fit with the job and organization. Like the whole selection process, the employment interview puts people in a situation where they see it as in their best interest to manage the impressions of the other party—even though they each hope to gain an unmanaged, independent impression for themselves.

That is, recruiters will promote their organization's status, reputation, and other advantageous features in efforts to ensure as large a pool as possible of qualified job candidates. Applicants want as many alternatives for jobs as possible, so they will present attractive impressions of themselves in various ways in an effort to impress interviewers and lead them to assessments of effective fit. At the same time, both recruiters and applicants are anxious to see through these attractive screens to what is really behind them—a devoted and enthusiastic worker or a slacker, an upbeat and rewarding workplace or a sweatshop. Or, in less invidious terms, a potential employee who will fit in and succeed in that particular workplace, and a workplace where the applicant will fit in and succeed. On each side, political skill promotes success.

These intentional efforts to manage the image of fit can lead decision makers to make wrong decisions. True fit is never completely knowable at this stage of the selection process, when little information is available to either side. Some might characterize such a decision context as "It's not what you are, it's what you appear to be."

Political Skill and Fit

Fit, as we've seen, is not well defined, difficult to precisely describe, and more of an intuitive hunch than a definitive thing. Decision makers really do struggle with their ability to clearly define what they mean by fit, but they usually can tell you when they run across either very good or very poor fit. It's that hard-to-explain quality, that *je ne sais quoi*, that is similar to the feeling they get when they encounter someone high in political skill. Indeed, we suggest that politically skilled individuals are apt to be perceived as fitting well with job and organization contexts. Those high in political skill possess the social astuteness and adaptability to assess the situation and formulate the proper influence strategy (the one that incorporates the proper methods of influence), and to execute it in an influential way that is perceived as genuine, sincere, and authentic.

The successful use of influence by politically skilled people, as noted in Chapter 1, is a result of two things:

- First, you need to accurately and astutely read the situation and select the proper influence tactic or strategy for that particular situation.

- Second, you need to execute the tactic or strategy in a convincing way that will lead to its success.

Efforts at interpersonal influence in the employment interview commonly take the form of ingratiation or self-promotion. Ingratiation is a tactic used to increase how much the interviewer likes you, and self-promotion is used to manage the interviewer's impressions of your competence. Job applicants often use either or both of these tactics to promote greater perceptions that they fit.

However, less skilled applicants tend to employ ingratiation when self-promotion is more appropriate. In fact, research on impression management in the employment interview has shown that applicants exhibiting ingratiation in the interview tend to be evaluated lower by interviewers than those who demonstrate self-promotion (for example, see Gilmore, Stevens, Harrell-Cook, & Ferris, 1999). The conclusion here—and one worth noting—is that discussing your strengths in an interview, if done with political skill, should enhance your chance of being hired over applicants who spend interview time complimenting the interviewer.

The informal rules of the game, and the implicit expectations in employment interviews, are that applicants are going to try to appear as talented, skilled, and qualified for the job as they possibly can. Interviewers usually expect people in these situations to self-promote. If an applicant goes against these expectations and does not self-promote but instead only tries to ingratiate, the effort might be interpreted as a character weakness in the applicant, that is, being too timid and perhaps even weak, resulting in lower evaluations from the interviewer.

So applicants have to size up the interview situation (determine the nature of the job they are applying for, the required skills and competencies, and what it will take to appear to fit this situation), and select the proper methods of influence. Politically skilled people usually know the proper tactics to employ in each situation. However, even when the proper tactics of influence are chosen, they won't be effective unless executed skillfully. People low in political skill may select influence tactics that are appropriate for a given situation; but they are likely to encounter difficulties when trying to execute influence effectively. For example, self-promotion can be tricky to manage. For each interviewer, there's an optimal level that is not so much that the applicant appears arrogant or conceited (as a society, we tend to despise arrogance and conceit), but also is not so little that the applicant seems weak or incompetent.

It's essential to gauge the level carefully, striving to demonstrate a level of self-promotion that identifies and presents your positive qualities in a confident rather than an obnoxious way. No one wants to hire a jerk! It is the individual who is high in political skill who will be able to fine-tune the execution of delivery in a way that achieves just the proper degree of social calibration— one that carefully strikes the proper balance and communicates just the right image: the image that fits.

Getting Hired by Getting Wired

The political skill of networking can also make a big difference in the hiring process. As noted in Chapter 1, networking ability involves the professional connections, alliances, coalitions, and friendships built up over time, which constitute social capital you can draw on when needed to exert influence. The adage "it is not what you know but who you know" contains a great deal of truth. Although this expression may be used cynically or realistically, and it comes across as a gross oversimplification, the fact of the matter is that some of both is needed—that is, what you know and who you know.

As you expand your professional network and are associated with influential others in important and meaningful ways, this conveys a strong and positive message about you and your abilities that can work to your advantage. Your networking ability and the resulting store of social capital can make it possible to call in favors, delicately mention influential names, and thus move to the front of the pack for job openings. Once again, politically skilled people will know precisely how to use such network information in an effective way, employing a subtle style that conveys an impressive image in an understated—never an offensive or over-bearing—way.

Research on Political Skill in the Employment Interview

Lest you think we're simply relying on intuitive hunches about the importance of political skill and how it should equip job applicants for the hiring process, here are reports of some research that has been conducted on the topic. Not surprisingly, political skill appears to be closely tied to success in the employment interview setting.

Corporate Recruiters

One study was conducted involving corporate recruiters from a number of different firms who were recruiting soon-to-be-graduates from a large midwestern university (Higgins, 2000). Students who registered with the placement office for on-campus interviews participated in the study, and they completed questionnaires measuring, among other things, their political skill. The recruiters who participated in the study completed questionnaires after their interviews with students, and they reported on how well they thought the student fit the job and the organization, and whether they would recommend that the student be hired and how positively they evaluated the student.

The results of the data analyses showed that job applicant political skill was significantly and positively related to recruiter assessments of both person-job fit and person-organization fit. Furthermore, political skill of job applicants was also significantly and positively related to hiring recommendations made by recruiters and to their overall positive evaluations of the job applicants.

Public Utility Interviewers

The other research investigation we found examining job applicant political skill and recruiter evaluations was set up a little differently (Gilmore & Ferris, 1989). Interviewers employed by a large public utility located in the southeastern United States participated in this research investigation as an exercise, part of a training and development program conducted on-site by one of the authors of the study. In this hiring exercise, interviewers were given the job description for a customer service representative position, along with a résumé that presented the woman applying for the job as either very qualified or very unqualified.

Then, all interviewers watched one of two videotaped employment interview segments featuring the applicant whose résumé they had assessed. Half of the interviewers saw an applicant who had been trained to display political skill: she made frequent eye contact, smiled frequently, showed feeling in answering questions from the off-camera interviewer, and demonstrated other behaviors in politically skilled ways. The other half of the interviewers saw an applicant who answered the questions without any feeling or emotion and who did not smile or demonstrate behaviors in any ways identifiable as politically skilled. Interviewers were then asked to evaluate their likelihood of hiring the candidate, how well she performed in the videotaped interview, and how well qualified she was for the job.

It turned out that the objective qualifications of the job applicant (which had been manipulated to appear either very strong or very weak for the job) had absolutely no effect on the evaluations. The only thing that made a difference was the applicant's political skill (or lack of), and it affected their likelihood of hiring her, the qualifications they perceived she had for the job, and how well they thought she performed in the interview.

Political Skill and Fit for Specific Hiring Targets

Political skill operates across the whole spectrum of employment. Here are two further examples, showing how it operates to establish fit in the hiring process for CEOs and college professors.

Hiring Corporate CEOs

Corporate chief executive officers set the vision and strategic plan for their organization. As a result, hiring the right CEO is perhaps the most critical decision an organization makes. The right CEO must not only be knowledgeable regarding the specific industry but also able to inspire trust, hope, and motivation in employees. Lee Iacocca's performance at Chrysler provides a vivid example of what this can mean. Iacocca has been called a "new kind of American icon—the celebrity CEO" (Marchica, 2004, p. 73).

John Marchica, a CEO himself, is very critical of some charismatic CEOs, asserting that they are responsible for talking up company stock to their employees but then dumping it themselves; he also points to disgraced top executives' trying to avoid responsibility and to the massive bankruptcies they manage to ride out. At the same time, he also acknowledges CEOs who have been able to turn companies around, such as Gerstner at IBM and Jobs at Apple, both of whom have the political skill needed to be successful but also the industry knowledge and personal fortitude to see the job through.

Political skill does not necessarily mean that leaders will be effective—they can be self-interested, even unethical. However, it is difficult to be effective without political skill. Thus, when hiring CEOs (or any top managers), it is important to consider their record for ethical behavior, their success, and their industry knowledge. Political skill should also be a primary factor in the hiring decision, just not the only factor. It can make the candidate's integrity, motivation, and industry knowledge likely to work well for the new employer.

Hiring University Professors

The personnel selection process for university professors usually involves a two-phase process of assessing fit:

First phase. The hiring university evaluates technical fit by considering the quality of the universities where the candidates received their Ph.D. degrees, the research publication records they have established, evidence of their teaching effectiveness, and the prominence and reputation of their various doctoral advisers (who provide recommendations). This technical aspect of fit might best be characterized as person-job fit, because it assesses the extent to which candidates possess qualifications for doing the job of professor. The outcome of the person-job-fit stage is the formation of a short list, say, three or four applicants who are invited for campus visits.

Second phase. In this phase, political skill tends to be what differentiates the short-listed candidates from one another. All the candidates invited for campus visits have passed the person-job-fit stage, and they all possess the skills to do the job. Therefore, the key consideration will be how well the candidates fit with the group of faculty in the department doing the hiring. Job candidates usually visit a campus for two days, during which time they participate in one-to-one meetings with individual faculty in the department; meetings with the Ph.D. students, usually as a group; a formal presentation of their research; and perhaps a meeting with the dean of the college and sometimes other administrators as well.

Besides these formal meetings, there are breakfasts, lunches, dinners, and possibly a reception at which interviewing and assessments of fit continue. These interactions might involve efforts to further assess the candidates' competencies, but the focus of the hiring department tends to center on these questions:

- Would the candidates be congenial colleagues?

- Does the faculty like them?

- Would the candidates be good organizational citizens? (That is, would they be willing to assume their fair share of departmental and college committee work, and so forth?)

Certainly, how the candidates conduct themselves, how they present themselves to faculty and students, and how astute and adaptable they are all go into the perceptions of fit the faculty forms of them. Therefore, politically skilled applicants stand out from less politically skilled but equally qualified candidates. Because competence was largely addressed in the first phase of fit, the second phase of fit focuses more on things such as liking and similarity to the group. Politically skilled job applicants are astute enough to read situations, gauge their audience, and calibrate their responses and behaviors socially in ways that facilitate the perception of high person-group fit—and thus solidify a job offer.

Conclusion

Getting hired in organizations today increasingly is determined by how well you fit the job, work group, or organization, but this notion of fit tends be poorly defined. Indeed, fit is usually some intuitive judgment or feeling by the person doing the hiring. Political skill arms you with the savvy to know just how to approach the hiring process, strategically select tactics of influence, execute them successfully, and win out in the competition for who fits the job best and gets hired. Once you're hired, you will be concerned about performing your job effectively and managing a successful career. Political skill plays a central role here as well, and that is the focus of the next chapter.

5

MAXIMIZING JOB
PERFORMANCE AND
CAREER SUCCESS

It almost goes without saying that organizations hire people to do specific jobs, and these days they spend a lot of time and money trying to predict which job candidates will perform best. The forward-looking among them also look for people with the potential to move on to greater things within the organization. If you get a job, clearly someone thought you could do well at it— and probably do well by it, too.

Some jobs call for great physical strength, and people incapable of heavy lifting don't stand a chance of being considered no matter how adept they are at interpersonal relations. Likewise, some jobs call for advanced skills in various realms of knowledge and technology, and again, political skill can't substitute for that kind of requirement. But many jobs involve working with and through other people—some as a primary requirement, and others where physical or technical abilities are required but not sufficient to get the job done. These jobs require political skill for effective performance.

This chapter presents the emerging evidence on how and why political skill serves as a good predictor of job performance. We explain what it means to perform a job effectively by focusing on the different criteria of job performance. Political skill is probably not going to make much difference on manual labor or machine operator jobs, where the important criterion may be something as simple as the number of parts produced. However, for most jobs, performance is assessed by a supervisor using somewhat subjective standards, and that is where interpersonal issues emerge and political skill can make a difference.

Building a record of consistently high job performance is important for securing rewards such as raises and promotions. Job performance is not the sole basis of the immediate or long-term rewards that make up overall career success, though. Your career is the collection of related positions, jobs, and experiences that defines your work identity over an extended period of time. And how you move or progress through those opportunities and jobs, how you get identified and labeled early on and thus become positioned well or badly to take advantage of opportunities—or create them—is a function of your political skill.

Political skill allows you to go beyond job performance to ensure success throughout your career. It is what puts you in a position to take advantage of opportunities presented to you, as well as to create opportunities of your own. Salary, promotions, and the attainment of prestigious positions are all indicators of career success, and they are all facilitated by political skill.

What Do We Mean by Job Performance?

The nature of job performance has fascinated managers and researchers alike for decades. Long after Munsterberg reformed Boston's hiring of railway motormen, the definition of job performance involved the tasks and duties that make up each job, and that was all. However, scholars studying performance at work have begun to recognize that job performance also has interpersonal and motivational aspects (Campbell, 1990)—catching up with the common observation that someone who is competent at the formal requirements of a job but makes other people's work harder can be a net loss for the organization.

Facets of Job Performance

So, as discussed in Chapter 1, we now make a distinction between task performance and contextual performance for almost all job types. Task performance is the set of tasks and duties central to a particular job—the things that differentiate one occupation from another. Contextual performance refers to behaviors inherent in all jobs that help maintain the social fabric of the organization: cooperating with others, helping out when not asked, following rules, persisting to finish an assignment, and so forth. Despite the different types of work behavior involved in the two types of performance, we have found that measures of political skill can often support predictions of which employees will receive high marks on either one.

Objective Versus Subjective Job Performance

Performance on the job can be measured in different ways, depending on the particular job in question. For machine operator jobs, one way to measure performance is to count the number of pieces of product produced per day. This is an objective measure of performance that involves no guesses, hunches, or opinions—just a straight physical tally. However, few jobs lend themselves to such neat, objective outcomes. Instead, organizations usually measure job performance by asking the immediate supervisor to rate the employee's performance, typically once a year. Most supervisors do the best they can, but performance ratings are inherently subjective. They capture lots of things besides how well an employee performed on the job: the kind of relationship between supervisor and employee, whether the supervisor likes the employee or not, what the supervisor thinks of the employee's potential for the future, and so forth. That means that performance ratings can be influenced by their subjects, and that opens the field to political skill.

What Does It Take to Perform Well on the Job?

The performance of an organization can be thought of as the aggregation of the individual performances of everyone in its workforce. Because companies are interested in having all their employees perform their jobs well, they spend a great deal of time and resources identifying the characteristics and qualities that support performance.

Current Screening Practice

Intelligence is the characteristic most commonly regarded as required for top performance on the job. Many believe that intelligence is a generally effective predictor of performance on all jobs (Schmidt & Hunter, 1998), and so you could do no better than to hire the smartest people for all jobs. However, in our view, intelligence may be quite important for some jobs, but other skills and abilities seem to make more difference for other jobs—and in some jobs, where the work is routine and requires little thought, intelligence may even be a disadvantage.

Further, intelligence on its own is often not enough for success. For example, managers need more than simple intelligence. In one overview of 151 studies published since World War II, the researchers found that intelligence was only modestly associated with leadership effectiveness (Judge, Colbert, & Ilies, 2004). They concluded that charisma and social skills, such as political skill, were most critical to leader effectiveness and success.

Personality is the predictor of job performance that has been investigated and found to indeed make a difference (Mount & Barrick, 1995). Conscientiousness, agreeableness, extroversion, openness to experience, and emotional stability (the "Big Five") are the traits most frequently considered, and they have demonstrated consistent relationships with job performance.

Personality traits generally are believed to be attributes you are born with, not easily shaped or developed. Also, if you possess a certain personality trait, or pattern of traits, the general view is that these traits become an important and defining part of your psychological makeup, and you are likely to demonstrate the behaviors associated with those traits in all work situations you encounter, whether they are called for or not. This might not match the changing demands of jobs in the contemporary work world.

Expanding the Field

As noted, the trend is to hire people to fit the organization, not just a specific job. The objective here is to select people who possess the set of qualities or competencies that will allow them to be equally effective in a variety of different jobs and work situations over a long period of time. In our view, intelligence and personality can be part of that set of desired competencies, but by no means are they the complete picture.

The work environments of today often are ambiguous and subject to constant change; they require employees who are socially astute, flexible, adaptable, and able to perform effectively through it all—that is, people who are politically skilled. Scholars and managers alike are becoming more aware of this: what is required to perform effectively in organizations is political will (the motivation and willingness to exercise influence) and political skill (the competency to execute such behavior).

It is important to remember that political skill is critical for success in any type of organization or group—corporations, nonprofit organizations, schools, small businesses, universities, hospitals, sports teams, voluntary organizations, even churches. When we interviewed Monsignor Connaughton, a prominent Catholic leader in New York City, he commented on the importance of networking to achieve goals: "In parish life, you need to have people around you—whether it's the parish council or the school advisory board—who come from different walks of life who have gifts and talents that they can offer to the parish. So if you are networking, you can find out, for example, who has the ability to advise us legally; who has the ability to advise us with maintenance; and who has the ability to help us through writing."

Further, Monsignor Connaughton argued that is it important for him to have political skill because he needs to adjust his behavior for different situations. Being flexible is an important aspect of his position; "I think one needs to be flexible because every day I'm going from one particular group with a specific need to another. For example, when I go to a hospital, I go from room to room and have people who are very receptive to my presence and other people not so receptive to my presence. So, although my behavior is consistent, flexibility comes in when I need to listen to someone who may have some anger to express against the Church. On the other hand, I might listen to someone who wants to tell me how wonderful the Church is or the experience of his or her parish. So, the flexibility and political skill has to do with my willingness to let the situation dictate to me how I should respond."

Regardless of the type of organization, as ambiguity and instability in work contexts increases, interpersonal or social factors—that is, political skill levels—play a greater and greater role in performance evaluations.

Political Skill and Performance Appraisal

Job performance measures the extent to which employees are *perceived* to be effective on the job, and perception can matter more than reality. In most jobs, as we noted, performance is assessed by someone's perception and subjective rating—usually the immediate supervisor, sometimes peers and co-workers, customers, or subordinates, all equally removed from objective measurement.

Consequently, in examining how political skill helps in job performance, we are actually considering how political skill helps in the perception of job performance by others, not real job performance. This inevitably allows for some nonperformance factors to enter into the evaluation process, which leads to a violation of one of the most central principles of performance appraisal: the job and its performance are being evaluated, rather than the performer in the abstract.

Ambiguity regarding the nature of performance increases as you move up the corporate hierarchy. Indeed, the very nature of managerial performance can be difficult to define with any precision. The key point is that whether or not observed work behaviors that substitute for direct measurement are really associated with effective performance, they can—with sufficient political skill—be manipulated to enhance the perception of effectiveness.

Effort and Goal Setting

Lacking objective measures of performance, managers attempt to rate employees by observing their attitudes, beliefs, values, and the effort they exhibit. One measure of effort sometimes used in this process is the set of performance-related goals employees set. Because these goals are indications of the effort to perform, if used skillfully and in sincere and convincing ways (that is, with political skill), goals can manage impressions of the supervisor conducting the evaluations in favorable ways. Indeed, research on performance appraisal has shown that regardless of how well employees subsequently performed on their jobs, the ones who set the highest goals received the highest performance ratings from their immediate supervisors (Frink & Ferris, 1998). Research here contradicts the common view that meeting a not-too-demanding goal is preferable to missing an ambitious one.

Politically skilled employees can set goals in ways that persuade their supervisors that they are ambitious, energetic, hardworking, committed, and doing all the right things—thus clearly leading to the conclusion that they must be effective performers.

In such cases, the effort reflected in the goals set tends to substitute for the goals met, and how well the employee actually does perform becomes largely irrelevant.

Perceived Similarity

Similarity breeds attraction, in everyday life and at work. The fact is that human beings generally feel most comfortable with those who seem most like themselves, and this similarity can be based on demographic characteristics like sex, race, and age, as well as on attitudes, beliefs, values, and positions taken on different issues. Supervisors are no more immune to this dynamic than anyone else, and it can easily creep into performance ratings. You probably can't do much to achieve physical resemblance to your boss—but with sufficient political skill, you can project images of similarity of attitudes, beliefs, and values, and that will influence your performance evaluation.

Take values: values have received much attention and consideration in corporate America in recent years. The most desirable employees share and live the core values proclaimed by their organizations. In many cases, the most important characteristic managers seek in their employees is appearing to think like the manager, make similar decisions, and support the manager on matters of importance. Reflecting such similarity leads to higher performance ratings and in-group status.

Managing perceptions of similarity in attitudes and beliefs is a delicate process that needs to be carefully considered and thoughtfully executed to be effective. An attempt to seem to hold similar views as the boss on all issues probably would not be effective. Instead, the botched attempt at influence would be seen as an effort to suck up to the boss. Political skill would enable you to read the boss and the context; determine which issues, beliefs, values, and so forth are most important to the boss; and convey an impression of agreement on enough of those to come across as the right kind of person. Additionally, the politically astute will realize that disagreeing with the boss occasionally can be helpful, but they will make sure it is on matters that are relatively unimportant to the boss.

Ingratiation and Self-Promotion

As noted, ingratiation and self-promotion are among the influence tactics people most often try to use in everyday life and in the job application process—and in the workplace itself. Some research on performance appraisal has found that the use of ingratiation and the use of self-promotion by employees led to quite different performance ratings from their supervisors because each tactic affected how much supervisors liked the employees.

Essentially, supervisors tended to like employees who used ingratiation, and in turn, assigned those employees higher performance ratings. The use of self-promotion toward supervisors not only did not help employees, it actually hurt them. Supervisors tended to dislike those employees who used self-promotion, and that dislike led them to give the employees lower performance ratings (Ferris, Judge, Rowland, & Fitzgibbons, 1994). And this tendency operated even when there were no real differences in the actual performance of the employees.

We believe that political skill is the triggering mechanism that explains the difference in outcomes. It doesn't matter how well you execute an influence tactic if it's the wrong thing to do at that time. Every context has an expected pattern of behavior, and astute individuals try to read situations and then conform their behavior to the demands or expectations implicit in them. Political skill will allow you to identify the proper pattern of behavior and then execute it appropriately—thus resulting in the construction of the proper image, which gets rated highly.

In the job application process, as described in Chapter 4, skillful self-promotion improves job applicants' prospects, whereas ingratiation actually hurts them. The performance appraisal context is just the reverse, and the people who fail to do well as a result probably lack the political skill to read the situation and identify the most appropriate influence strategy.

The implicit rules of engagement in the employment interview, where interviewers typically have never met the job applicants and know little about them, say that self-promotion is appropriate and approved, and ingratiation by applicants is seen as timidity and weakness of character. However, the performance appraisal appears to have different implicit rules. The participants share a history and interact on an ongoing basis in a work relationship, and the supervisor has quite a bit of information about the employee.

When doing performance appraisals, it is difficult to disentangle the work relationship and personal feelings from performance ratings. Work relationships obviously will progress more positively if they are characterized by liking rather than dislike. Job applicants are expected to toot their own horns; employees are not—supervisors will read it as arrogance or conceit. Politically skilled employees realize this. They not only identify the most appropriate pattern of behavior to demonstrate but execute it in ways that appear genuine and sincere, which typically yields positive outcomes.

Also, some behaviors are naturally interpreted (particularly if not executed well) as more overt, almost to the point of overkill, whereas others are more subtle. To be influential, you have to appear *not* to be trying to exercise influence, and certainly not for personal gain. Those who engage inappropriately in self-promotion, being low in political skill, are likely to come across as manipulative, whereas those who engage in well-placed ingratiation come across as subtle, nonmanipulative, and humble, and thus are likelier to gain reward.

Political Skill and Job Performance: Research Results

Because scales or measures of political skill have been available for such a short time, little research has been conducted to assess the role political skill plays either in the workplace in general or in job performance in particular. However, a couple of recent studies do seem to confirm our predictions about political skill and job performance ratings.

One study (reported in Ferris et al., 2005) examined the political skill and job performance of branch managers of a national financial services firm. Managers completed the *Political Skill Inventory*, and scores were computed and correlated with annual performance ratings on the managers provided by their immediate supervisors. The managers were rated on twenty-eight categories of performance that ranged from "budgeted revenue growth" to "interpersonal relationships." The results of statistical analyses showed that even after controlling for a number of variables, participants' political skill was significantly and positively related to the job performance ratings they received from their supervisors. Therefore, it appears from this study that the more politically skilled managers received higher performance ratings.

Another study was conducted on the political skill and job performance of managers from a large motor manufacturing company in Australia (Semadar, 2004). In this study, managers were assessed on political skill using the PSI measure, and they also completed measures of emotional intelligence, leadership self-efficacy, and self-monitoring. When these four measures were analyzed at the same time for their impact on job performance ratings, political skill was found to be the strongest predictor of positive performance ratings; political skill also strongly differentiated managers assigned to the highest performance rating category from those assigned to other categories.

So, although the evidence is still limited, political skill appears to play an important role in job performance—a role by no means limited to contextual performance, to the interpersonal behaviors that help the organization in general. A compelling argument can be made that political skill is so fundamental to all jobs that it should be a strong predictor of both task and contextual dimensions of supervisor-rated job performance.

Political skill affects the quality and quantity of work (that is, core task performance) in jobs where work is accomplished with the assistance of others. For example, workers high in political skill are likely to be more effective than those low in political skill at facilitating the cooperative work-related activities necessary to maintain the quality of their output.

Political skill also affects perception of job dedication, because politically skilled employees are likely to be more effective than those low in political skill in demonstrating behaviors that create an image of following rules and demonstrating commitment and motivation. Similarly, because politically skilled employees can astutely assess situations and demonstrate appropriate emotion control and influence, they may be better at dealing patiently with difficult customers and co-workers and at influencing others. Therefore, political skill should also affect the interpersonal facilitation facet of job performance.

Socially effective individuals, like those high in political skill, are better able to meet the demands of most environments by adjusting their actions to the most appropriate level, which seems to suggest a strong link between political skill, adaptability, and performance. Furthermore, adaptable individuals have been found to deal more effectively and be more comfortable operating in real-world domains (Block & Kremen, 1996). Interestingly, individuals with high intelligence or cognitive ability scores but low adaptability were less able to initiate and develop positive social interactions.

Politically skilled employees are able to develop appropriate behaviors and adjust those behaviors to different work contexts while also using effective emotion control and regulation. Research has indicated that demonstrating favorable emotions at work, a behavior consistent with high political skill, translates into not only higher achievement but greater allocation of rewards by others: employees displaying positive emotions at work were more likely to receive higher performance evaluations from their supervisors (Staw & Barsade, 1993).

What Do We Mean by Career Success?

For most people in the workplace, getting ahead is something for which they work very hard, and it means career success. Career success is usually indicated by the promotions individuals receive and the salary levels they achieve over the course of a career. Because pay is typically linked to job level, the pay most people receive depends on their promotion, transfer, or reassignment to jobs higher up the company ladder.

Of course, the nature of promotion is changing as companies downsize, restructure, and generally become flatter, with fewer layers in the corporate hierarchy. Flatter organizations provide fewer openings for traditional promotion. Also, companies are changing their views on how quickly employees should be promoted, moving from a fast-track philosophy to one of somewhat slow-track evaluations and promotions, with longer expected time in each position. Promotions will continue to be made, but other types of recognition will grow in importance: perhaps reassignment to interesting, challenging, and prestigious roles or team projects, which may not constitute actual promotion but will still be viewed as a reward.

We believe that in internal contests for attractive and prestigious positions, employees will come out much better if they have political skill. Politically skilled individuals will be able to position themselves to create opportunities as well as to take advantage of opportunities presented to them. As we have noted, political skill is not influence by brute force. Quite the opposite, political skill involves the subtle and often indirect influence over others that is accomplished with a combination of a sincere and trustworthy style, the capacity to astutely read situations and flexibly adapt behavior accordingly, and to apply social capital (networks, connections, and the like) effectively.

Much as good rebounders in basketball seem to know just where to go to capitalize on the angle the ball takes off the rim or backboard, politically skilled individuals seem to know the importance of positioning and make sure they are where they can take advantage of opportunities. They accomplish this by reading others effectively and positioning themselves both for one-to-one interpersonal influence and in networks that give them access to information and resources. They also use their understanding of the importance of receiving mentoring or sponsorship to keep themselves visible for any opening that appears.

Factors Determining Career Success

Political skill plays a role in all the main indicators of career success. Whether you're looking at promotions, pay and compensation levels, or job survival, the politically skillful come out ahead.

Promotions

Promotions are among the most political decisions made in organizations. Part of the difficulty with promotion systems is that the requirements or criteria for promotion may not be clearly specified. Managers generally wind up looking for people who fit best or show the most potential, or both; but *fit* and *potential* probably mean something different to each manager making promotion decisions. Most of the time, the definitions actually in use involve remarkable similarity to the characteristics and qualities of the manager in question. This process certainly seems to have been the dominant promotion model in organizations for quite some time. Unfortunately, it reduces variation among promoted individuals.

It has been long recognized that if you have what it takes to do the next job up, then the real key to being promoted is to make sure you get noticed. Economics provides the useful concept of *market signaling theory* (Spence, 1974), which describes the use of individual activities or attributes to convey information and alter the beliefs of others in a given market. Although the original theory tended to focus on characteristics such as education and experience, it could be expanded to focus on things such as reputation, ability, and fit. Political skill is what allows you to transmit such information in subtle ways—not trumpeting your achievements but nonetheless making sure that your talents attract the attention of important top managers and decision makers.

Tournament theory is another useful way of considering promotions and mobility in organizations. A tournament is a way of identifying the most qualified candidate for a position by pitting individuals against one another in increasingly selective competitions. At each stage along the way, decisions are made regarding winners and losers; in a decided labeling process, winners are seen as stars and progress to the next stage, whereas losers are stigmatized and diverted to a losers' bracket. Winners gain higher positions, more attention from managers, additional training and development, access to privileged information, and—perhaps most important—an expectation that they will continue to be winners. Meanwhile, losers suffer lower status and reduced rewards and an expectation of being unlikely to do well in the future.

Tournament theory seems to imply that winners of competitions are declared on some sort of objective basis, as if there were clearly specified criteria for winning. In fact, this does not appear to be the case. Promotion criteria are not clearly stated (or not stated at all), and decisions are highly subjective and thus quite susceptible to influence and manipulation. Furthermore, although sports tournaments devote much attention to the bracketing process and the levels and stages of play, work organizations have only one really critical round: the first one, when impressions of candidates are formed that carry into the future and can influence future opportunities provided to winning candidates. The attention and resources allocated to initial winners can actually result in their becoming the best candidates further up the hierarchy (for example, see Cooper, Graham, & Dyke, 1993).

Politically skilled employees are best positioned to take advantage of signaling theory, as well as to compete effectively in the organization's unannounced tournaments for promotion. The general and ill-defined characteristics of fit and potential that so often drive promotion decisions can be easily used by the politically skilled. However, even when a firm lays out more specific criteria or desired characteristics in its management succession system, the system still appears to work to the advantage of individuals with political skill. A survey of some Fortune 500 firms regarding the characteristics desired in those considered for promotion included the following: interpersonal skills, self-awareness, trustworthiness, character, empathy, street smarts, personal credibility, charisma, flexibility, influencing others, and integrity. When you throw all these things into the hopper, what do you have? Political skill!

As with performance ratings, promotion decisions tend to turn on perceived similarity with characteristics of the decision makers. Likewise, the skillful use of ingratiation tends to help career success, but self-promotion hurts. For example, one study of life at General Motors pointed out that managers' chance of promotion was determined by how skillfully they flattered their boss (Wright, 1979).

It takes effective political skill to employ assertiveness well in organizations—particularly in the context of promotion decisions, where influence is being directed upward. Any awkwardness or misplaced timing will likely be perceived as inappropriately controlling for someone in a subordinate position. We have observed assertiveness on the part of promotion candidates lead to lower evaluations of their promotability, which implies that the tactic was not appropriate for the situation or was not executed well, either of which would indicate a lack of political skill.

To be promoted, you need a record of effective performance in the organization, but such a record is not sufficient. In addition, you need political skill. The two together make an unbeatable combination, but separately, each can lead to an early career ceiling. You can perform well and fail if you are not politically skilled. You can have excellent political skills and fail if you make sufficiently disastrous or frequent technical errors. However, even if your performance is average, you can be considered an insider with potential to advance if you are seen as politically skilled.

The network-building facet of political skill also contributes in important ways to career success. It seems intuitively obvious that having a vast network can improve career outcomes, but the mechanism has been difficult to define. Scott Seibert and his associates (Seibert, Kraimer, & Liden, 2001) recently made some headway on this point. They examined how network connections and social capital accumulation operated to enhance career success and found that the alliances, coalitions, and contacts people build up as parts of their network lead to greater access to information, resources, and sponsorship (or mentoring). These resources in turn lead to greater promotions, salary, and general career success.

Although most people like to believe that ability drives the promotion process, and ability really is what companies seek, in practice it seems to be crowded out by factors favoring those high in political skill. When all the candidates have adequate ability, qualities like the ability to get along well with others loom large in the decision. Also, being perceived as a team player is important, and politically skilled persons will pick up signals from their bosses and other influential players in the work environment that indicate the right things to do and say at the right time to show themselves to best advantage.

As you move to higher levels in the corporate hierarchy, variability on intelligence, past work experience, and performance narrows considerably; because everybody looks about the same on these qualities, they are not going to be the bases for promotion decisions. *Style* differentiates winners from losers at the upper levels, and style is what we refer to as political skill. Furthermore, it is how you manage the impressions that your style is similar to, and fits with, the style of the managers making the promotion decisions that will lead to success.

Overall, we believe political skill positions people to be competitive and successful in the promotion process. Political skill can give you visibility, distinguish you favorably from others, and get you promoted. Because of massive organizational change, restructuring and design, promotion systems are going to be ever more constrained, and political skill correspondingly ever more essential as you make your way to the top.

Pay and Compensation

Decisions about employee pay and compensation tend to be mired in politics, and reasons other than merit and performance often influence their outcomes. Research has shown that effective use of ingratiation helps salary progression (Gould & Penley, 1984). What other researchers (Kipnis & Schmidt, 1988) called a "tactician" approach to influence (the strategic selection of only the most appropriate influence tactics) resulted in higher salaries than those obtained by employees who used the contrasting "shotgun" approach (an indiscriminant use of many influence tactics). Ingratiation implies appearing pleasant and trying to be liked, and it probably leads to favorable outcomes for politically skilled people who execute it well because of the liking it inspires. Other research has shown that the demonstration of positive emotional responses by employees in the workplace favorably affects the pay they receive (Staw, Sutton, & Pelled, 1994).

Also, political connections, part of the networking facet of political skill, were associated with higher pay raises, but only when employees emphasized the dependency of their manager or superior on them (Bartol & Martin, 1990). This dependency effect is an interesting one, and a strategy that politically skilled people often employ to maximize both salary and promotion possibilities. Politically skilled people work hard at positioning themselves in a number of ways, but one way is to become indispensable to the boss, so the boss's effectiveness depends on their continuing service. If a boss who is talented and obviously going places learns to depend on you, you will go along for the ride as the boss rises in the organization, receiving attractive promotions and salary increases along the way.

A final issue concerning political skill and pay concerns the usually controversial topic of CEO compensation, which leads people to question the basis of such big ticket decisions. Boards of directors represent shareholders and, among other duties, are accountable for conducting performance evaluations of CEOs and for negotiating increases in compensation (which may include components such as base salary, bonus, stock, and perks).

In theory, boards are independent entities, so that they can view CEO behavior objectively and render unbiased evaluations of performance and determinations of compensation. But that has not been the case in many organizations over the years. Instead, a close and complex relationship often develops between the CEO and board members, a relationship that is strategically managed by politically skilled CEOs. Despite formal procedures for selecting new members to serve on boards and for other board procedures, the CEO often proposes new members and orchestrates support from existing board members.

Remember that board members are paid stipends to serve, receive expenses and meeting fees, and in some companies also receive generous perks. In light of this special treatment, compliments of the CEO, it is quite difficult for board members to be truly objective in the performance evaluations and salary determinations of their benefactor. It is a power and patronage relationship, carefully and thoughtfully orchestrated by skilled CEOs, and it leads to higher pay. The power involved is almost never blatant, direct, and overbearing; boards have their limits. Instead, CEOs successful at this process employ great political skill, applying their social capital, reputation, and the positioning that these assets produce to ensure a favorable outcome for themselves.

Political Skill and Job Survival

We have seen a number of top politicians ruin their careers over bad choices or bad personal decisions. But few have managed to survive as well as Bill Clinton did in the wake of the Monica Lewinsky scandal that almost dislodged him from the Oval Office.

Clinton, with his seemingly sincere plea for forgiveness, his heartfelt apology to his family, friends, staff, cabinet, and the Lewinsky family, as well as his willingness to take responsibility (albeit a long time after the fact) were all done in a very politically skilled way. Apologizing and asking forgiveness works only if you do it right—and Clinton knows how to do it right. Regardless of whether he actually felt these emotions—and who is to say he did not feel them?—he was convincing to many. Again, it is not only what you do but how you do it that leads to success and survival!

Further, Clinton knows how to network (a dimension of political skill) and with whom. As the press began to ask questions about impeachment and resignation, Clinton went out and got support from high-profile religious and work leaders, such as the Reverend Bernice King (Martin Luther King Jr.'s daughter) and Nelson Mandela. King and Mandela praised his work and asked Congress and the American people for tolerance and forgiveness.

In *My Life* (2004), Clinton wrote, "As good as Mandela was, the Reverend Bernice King . . . stole the show. She said that even great leaders sometimes commit grievous sins; that King David had done something far worse than I had in arranging the death in battle of Bathsheba's husband, who was David's loyal soldier, so that David could marry her; and that David had to atone for his sin and was punished for it. No one could tell where Bernice was going until she got to the closing: 'Yes, David committed a terrible sin and God punished him. But David remained king.'" Clearly, Clinton's networking and the political skill of his supporters were crucial to his continued presidency. These same principles—social astuteness, interpersonal influence, networking ability, and apparent sincerity—come into play for people trying to survive in any organization.

Sometimes organizations reach a point where they believe they must terminate employees for a variety of reasons, which typically include poor job performance, deteriorating financial performance of the firm that dictates downsizing, or simply what are known as irreconcilable differences with the boss. Some employees encounter these situations and lose their jobs, others keep them. We believe that political skill often makes the difference—survivors are those who persuade their employer that performance deficiencies can be made up, that others are less valuable and thus better let go in a general downsizing, or that the irreconcilable can be reconciled after all.

Despite universities' efforts to prepare graduates for the work world, it looks as though they could be doing a better job of instilling the political realities of work environments. The incidence of job failure for managers and executives taking new positions is much higher than you might expect: about 40 percent fail and are terminated within the first eighteen months. The most cited reasons for such job failure included "being unclear about what bosses want, inability to make tough decisions, being unable to build partnerships with subordinates and peers, and lack of political savvy" ("Up and out: Rude awakenings come early," 1995, p. 3). Additionally, the Chicago outplacement firm of Challenger, Gray, and Christmas found that "getting along with the boss is more important than job performance in surviving a corporate cutback" ("Job security: Collect those brownie points," 1996, p. 3).

This all seems to highlight the realization that job survival may depend more on your political skill than just about anything else. In downsizing, companies sometimes apply a decision rule to dictate that a certain department or unit will be cut or dropped entirely. However, in many cases, there is no decision rule, and then it can be hard to tell what determines who stays and who goes—but the decisions probably involve politics and judgments of fit. In unclear situations, top management may try to downsize in a way that preserves some sense of harmony, perhaps looking for a particular fit in those who will remain.

Politically skilled employees can manage that fitting-in process by demonstrating the extensiveness of their connections and networks with influential others and units, emphasizing key competencies that make them indispensable to the boss and organization, and drawing on the effective and friendly working relationship they have carefully cultivated with the boss.

Conclusion

Performance ratings and career success for most jobs in organizations today are determined increasingly by working smarter, not just harder, and demonstrating the ability to meet your goals working with and through others. For most jobs, no one is counting widgets to measure performance; instead, your boss is rating your performance based on your capacity to be influential and effective at what you do. This makes political skill one of the most important competencies you can possess if you wish to maximize not just your day-to-day job performance but also your long-term career success. Very much involved in the process of building a record of effective job performance and establishing a successful career is the concept of reputation, or what you are and become known for in the eyes of others. Chapter 6 develops the point that political skill is also a key ingredient in the formation and maintenance of your reputation at work.

6

Enhancing Your Reputation

Your reputation is made up of the qualities and actions that others know you for. You can have more than one reputation—as a friend, a business associate, a family member—but within the area where it applies, your reputation makes a big difference in your ability to influence others. And, as in so many other aspects of community life, political skill turns out to be a key factor in the development, maintenance, and defense of reputation.

This chapter focuses on what goes into the reputation you have on the job. We outline the qualities, characteristics, and behaviors that contribute to your personal reputation and thus shape your influence and effectiveness at work.

What Is Reputation?

Reputation can be a neutral term, denoting any reasonably widespread views of a person or thing, whether favorable or not. However, it is often used interchangeably with positive terms such as *standing, prestige,* and *status* (all typically assumed to be *high* unless otherwise qualified), and as an opposite to negative terms such as *infamy.*

Your reputation is a form of identity made up of a complex combination of perceived characteristics and accomplishments, demonstrated behaviors, and intended images presented over a period of time. It exists separately in the mind of each observer, as observed directly or as reported from secondary sources. Thus reputation has two broad aspects: performance or getting things done, and perceived character and integrity. Additionally, the concept of an identity implies that you can potentially have a number of different, even conflicting, reputations, each identified and interpreted by a different constituent target individual or group.

Note that *reputation* as we define the term denotes something based on perception and subjective in nature, thus defined in the eye of the beholder. This definition suggests that reputation is influenced by personal characteristics (including uncontrollable aspects such as sex, race and ethnicity, age, and so on) that can serve as signals or proxies for reputation. At the same time, another important part of the definition has to do with deliberate accomplishments and developed characteristics such as political skill, which can help shape your reputation in each part of your life.

Finally, we note that various aspects of personal behavior and decisions can come together in complex ways to create reputation. Particularly with positive reputations, it appears that the combination of these elements can be greater than the simple sum of the individual parts. Indeed, we would argue further that well-developed reputations can be very difficult (if not impossible) to imitate or copy.

As a result, reputation is an intangible resource that can reflect value and represent a source of sustained competitive advantage for an individual or an organization—or destroy it.

Consider the case of Lee Iacocca, former chairman and CEO of the Chrysler Corporation. His reputation as a visionary and savvy business manager has brought him great wealth, consistent employment, and international acclaim, not to mention celebrity status. His amazing turnaround of Chrysler was done largely on the force of his political skill and reputation. His unique and powerful business reputation not only benefited him as an individual but also enhanced the status and influence of any organization aligned with him. He produced results, and he was reputed to be a man of integrity, strong values, and ethical principles, the two sets of components we tend to see in reputations. Now contrast Iacocca with "Chainsaw" Al Dunlap, former CEO of the Sunbeam Corporation. He was known for improving the performance numbers of corporations he led, but his prickly personality and lack of political skill contributed to a reputation as unreasonable and unethical, and also untrustworthy, which contributed to his business demise.

Ingredients of Reputation

Reputation is a complex of individual qualities and known accomplishments that can be classed as forms of capital: human capital, political capital, social capital. These three categories combine differently to form each reputation, merging in complex ways and weighted according to the context where the reputation applies. No two contexts are exactly the same, so no one can duplicate a reputation by duplicating the actions of its holder.

Human Capital

According to human capital theory, individuals generate increased worth or value for themselves by acquiring knowledge, skills, and credentials through education and experience. For example, earning an advanced degree contributes to your human capital, and the prestige of the institution granting the degree can enhance (or decrease) the value of that contribution. Job knowledge and experience also build human capital, as do skills acquired through training. Studies have indicated that factors such as age, race, and sex can affect the return on investments made in human capital.

As a component of reputation, human capital represents investments made by individuals to enhance their public image. In the form of credentials, human capital provides instant credibility and status—the framed diploma is a traditional symbol of an independent professional at work. Similarly, certain individual characteristics ranging from job experience to manner and bearing can make an individual more marketable and mobile.

Because lifetimes are finite, age has to be considered in any discussion concerning the value of human capital. The timing of investments in human capital is a factor in the resulting value; early investments in education and training are likely to yield greater lifelong returns; thus, a younger person would be expected to have greater long-term potential. Alternatively, age serves as a proxy for experience, so an older person will be perceived as being more experienced and potentially more valuable for an immediate need.

Education and experience are both components of an individual's reputation that are affected by age, but the relationship is not always linear. As an example, take Steve Jobs in his career at Apple computer. Early on in his career, Jobs had a reputation as a business visionary that far exceeded his age counted either as years of education or of experience. In contrast, former IBM CEO John Akers had a reputation that developed over time as a rather linear combination of age and experience.

From the human capital perspective, sex and race have strong implications for reputation. These characteristics are often taken as proxies for your actual qualifications; they become part of your human capital. These characteristics might operate directly as well as interactively with other characteristics to add to your reputation.

Political Capital

Reputation is influenced by personal characteristics and therefore reflects your intelligence, personality, and political skill, all of which build political capital. Furthermore, as noted in Chapter 1, networking ability—an important facet of political skill—leads to the development and accumulation of social capital, which also is a key ingredient in reputation. Personal characteristics influence how people are perceived and evaluated in work settings, as well as how they perform various aspects of their work roles. We identify and discuss representative constructs in this area, rather than conducting a comprehensive or exhaustive examination.

Two personal characteristics with the most influence on reputation are intelligence and personality. We believe intelligence influences reputation insofar as it guides and facilitates job performance effectiveness. Personality (particularly the trait referred to as conscientiousness) also influences reputation through its effects on job performance and work behavior. Collectively, then, intelligence and personality affect political capital mainly through the effects they have on job performance.

Political skill is the key aspect or ingredient in political capital, and it contributes to reputation in important ways that involve influence over the impressions others form. It also contributes by way of the social capital that accumulates as a result of network-building efforts. The ability to read, understand, and control perceptions and social interactions at work is absolutely critical to getting things done, and thus to building a favorable reputation. In addition, politically skilled people inspire trust and confidence, which are also critical elements in the development of a reputation, in others around them.

Because your reputation forms over time, when you first enter an organization, managing the early interactions with others and the image you project is important for subsequent interactions and impressions. Initial impressions are lasting, and they affect how others behave. Politically skilled individuals are well aware of this, and they make immediate efforts to come across as influential. If others perceive you as influential, they will be more likely to treat you as such, granting you more latitude and challenging or attacking you less often and less strongly, which will allow you to actually accomplish more, all of which will further enhance your reputation for being influential, effective, and powerful.

Building favorable reputations in organizations relies on political competence, positioning, and savvy. Additionally, the social understanding and influence components of political skill, combined with the network-building or social capital enhancement facet, have been found to be fundamental to the success of entrepreneurs (Baron & Markman, 2000). Political skill has also been identified as an especially vital component of women's career advancement (Mainiero, 1994).

Political skill seems to promote and enhance reputation by enabling workers to navigate political environments and influence others in the work setting. As responsibilities increase, particularly in managing and leading others, political skill may be the factor that does most to smooth your way upward. To the degree that navigating organizational politics and influencing others are critical factors in managerial success, political skill is what will help you build a reputation for savvy and for the leadership influence that is so valued in organizations today.

Social Capital

Within organizations, the value of a reputation is strongly influenced by relationships and the influence wielded through those relationships. Networking ability is the facet of political skill that develops the alliances, coalitions, and friendship networks that build social capital. If social influence is the process by which you directly or indirectly influence others, then social capital represents a latent form of social influence based on the availability of social contact and network resources.

The mix of human capital, political skill, and social networking helps define the personal reputations of organization members. Social capital enhances reputation by conveying information concerning credibility that people use to make judgments. And social capital, through network development, access to information, resources, and mentoring, has been positively related to career success (Seibert et al., 2001). To the extent that you can build a reputation for being successful in your career, the development of networks and use of the social capital in these networks can enable such success. Access to resources is often granted based on personal contact and mutual trust, and trust tends to develop over time as part of your reputation within the various networks you draw on.

Social capital also has been linked to voluntary turnover in organizations, whereby the strength of one person's social capital leads to strong network ties. If the central figure of such a network departs, the others tend to follow—and the organization suffers. Positioning yourself so that you are known to have the ability and desire to take care of those in your network will draw others to you, which can further develop your social capital and reputation (Dess & Shaw, 2001).

How Reputation Is Communicated

As sociologist Erving Goffman (1959) pointed out almost half a century ago, everyday life can be regarded as a series of individual theatrical performances whereby people seek to control others through a projected image. It is especially useful to think of life in organizations as made up such performances, with members all presenting themselves in ways designed to guide and control the perceptions that others form of them.

Signaling theory provides further insight into organizational life, as it expands on the notion of a theatrical performance and provides a useful perspective from which to consider reputations. As outlined by A. Michael Spence (1974), signaling theory suggests that individuals coexist in markets of exchange, and within these markets, individuals signal others in the market in an attempt to convey information or alter their beliefs. Spence classed any characteristic of an individual that could be observed by others and altered by the individual as a potential signal. In his view, a potential signal became an actual signal if it did exercise an influence on others. From this perspective, reputation can be regarded as an actual signal because it does influence others.

Focusing on the alterable aspect of a signal suggests that reputation can be an intentional effort at signaling, shaped or influenced by the individual to whom the reputation refers. Building a reputation quickly is especially valuable, because—as tournament theory indicates—those who experience early advancement are likely to find greater success over the course of their careers. Tournament theory clearly supports the idea of reputation as a signal to decision makers, whereby fast-track employees are identified and subsequently promoted based on their reputations of early success.

How Reputations Evolve

Reputations evolve mostly through two distinct processes: development and maintenance. A third process—defense—will be called for whenever the threat of potential damage arises. The time frames surrounding development and maintenance are likely to differ widely as a function of both personal and contextual factors, so it is impossible to predict or advise anyone about moving from one process to another. Furthermore, it is certainly possible and even likely that the two processes often overlap for any given individual, and—though everyone hopes to avoid the necessity—can defer to the necessities of defense at any time. Nonetheless, all three repay analysis as separate entities.

Reputation Development

To build a reputation, you need to amass human capital in the form of credentials and history, establish social capital such as networks and interpersonal relationships that are valued within the specified context, and develop political capital to take advantage of these assets. Additionally, what people see you do must match or exceed what they expect from you.

Here's an example: Tim McGraw is a country musician with ambitions to run for the U.S. Senate. And he's well on the way. *Time* (September 20, 2004, pp. 71–72) calls him "The Clinton of Country" because of his political skill. Though most musicians dread the pre-concert compulsory meet-and-greet sessions with local fans, DJs, and children of corporate sponsors, Tim McGraw loves them. *Time* describes him as shaking everyone's hand and being able to charm people more or less regardless of the circumstances. All this helps him maintain his reputation in the country music industry, of course, but he's also looking beyond that and gently reminding people that he has larger interests. Through the election season, he closed each gig with "As Americans, you have a responsibility to vote, so get out there and do it." Watch for his name; he's using his place and reputation in the music industry to begin building a reputation as someone who cares about America, democracy, and government, and you may well see him representing his state of Tennessee on a national stage.

Reputation Maintenance

Maintaining a reputation requires that what others see you do must remain consistent with what they expect. Any inconsistency, positive or negative, will result in adjustments to your reputation, which in turn redefine the context and the perceptions of your human, political, and social capital. Unlike developing a reputation, however, maintaining a reputation mainly involves simply being aware of the reputation and acting in accordance with the behaviors prescribed by it.

Jim Moran, chairman of Southeast Toyota Distributors, is arguably the most successful automobile dealer in the world. His company is a $3.5 billion private corporation, yet Jim carefully maintains his reputation as a "regular guy"—after all, that reputation helped get him where he is today. Jim began his career working at a gas station in Chicago. He saved enough money to buy a Sinclair gas station for $360 and turned it into the chain's most profitable station in the Chicago area. When he was diagnosed with cancer in the 1960s, he decided to retire to Florida. His retirement did not last long; his cancer went into remission and Jim started Southeast Toyota when he was in his early fifties. His humble beginnings and blue-collar background are part of who he is today. He still has weekly lunches with employees ranging from top management and division heads to maintenance workers and clerical staff. Everyone gets the opportunity to have lunch with Moran. His reputation of being a regular guy is enhanced by his appreciation for others in his company—he comes across as a generous man who values the work of others.

We don't mean to imply that all maintenance behaviors are merely behaviors that conform to the reputation. Indeed, contexts are constantly changing, thus requiring a continuous calibration of the reputation. Maintaining a reputation involves anticipating and perceiving future changes in context, as well as protecting and defending the existing reputation. For a similar dynamic, see Mark Suchman's (1995) strategies for maintaining legitimacy.

Reputations necessarily are nested within a particular context, and though they may initially transfer to a new context, aggressive maintenance or even development may be needed to reaffirm or establish the reputation in the new context. For example, if you were promoted from a lower level in the organization based on your reputation within that level, people would take you on faith for a while. If you failed to perceive the new context accurately and live up to the new expectations, however, you would probably soon see your reputation decline.

Reputation Defense

Reputation, no matter how arduously constructed and painstakingly maintained, is fragile. It can take a lifetime to build and a moment to destroy—consider the rapid fall from the national spotlight suffered by Representatives Newt Gingrich and Gary Condit, Senator Bob Packwood, and corporate executives like

Kenneth Lay, Bernie Ebbers, and Dennis Kozlowski. Networks don't just convey and enhance reputations, they serve as enforcers as well—behave badly toward any one member of a network and it will be reported to the rest, which puts a premium on maintaining the expected level of benevolent support. Likewise, sending mixed or false signals to a network can be devastating to reputation and credibility; people lose confidence in your subsequent marketing signals, and this loss lingers for a long time.

Defense of a reputation may be called for following an unfortunate event or a deliberate attempt to damage the reputation. You have to be alert for potential damage and deliberate attacks, because no matter how often people decry the behavior, damaging a competitor's reputation by way of criticism, misinformation, distortion, or rumor works. Putting the other guy down is known to be an effective way to advance in an organization.

We need look no further than our legal system to see defense of reputations in action. As David Logan (2001) points out, from 1980 to 2000, courts awarded more than $620 million to plaintiffs suing the media for damage to personal reputations. However, Logan also notes that this figure is misleading and does not account for individuals unwilling to endure proceedings that put their reputation under close scrutiny. This implies that although some people will defend their reputations vigorously, others concede that the defense is more costly than developing a new reputation. Some have suggested that the best defense of a reputation is an active offense—using aggressive maintenance behaviors and keeping a close eye on changes in context to help prevent a crisis (Fombrun, 1996).

Some subscribe to the maxim "when something goes wrong, the first thing you fix is the blame." Such individuals try to defend their reputations by structuring and manipulating perceptions formed by others concerning the causes of their good and poor performance. The idea is that what people think about the reasons for a problem will affect the way they act toward those involved in it.

When incidents of poor performance occur at work, the people involved usually engage in active efforts to influence the meaning attributed to the incident—and to reduce their perceived responsibility for whatever went wrong. They can employ a number of defensive tactics, including excuses, apologies, and justifications, to reshape perceptions of the incident. The politically skillful know just which tactics to employ and how to execute them in convincing ways that absolve them of any wrongdoing.

Organizations sometimes employ image management tactics. Corporate annual reports and shareholder letters carefully position top management to take credit for successful performance while attributing any poor performance to unforeseen factors in the external environment.

Although we see political skill as a positive thing, it can be used in negative ways—such as when managers doctor corporate annual reports to absolve themselves of responsibility for failure. Incidents of poor performance call for language that persuasively and convincingly distances management from responsibility for any negative outcomes. To succeed, such rhetorical masterpieces must be created by managers whose highly developed political skill has fueled the creation of unquestionable reputations characterized by high levels of trust and sincerity.

Importance of Reputation

Reputations at work are important and valuable commodities, and they are developed over time through active and politically skilled efforts by individuals to influence how they are perceived and known by others. Political skill and social capital combine with human capital to serve as the key ingredients in a reputation. The larger your resources and the greater your access to information—and the more influential your friends and colleagues are seen to be—the more favorable the reputation you will have. And your access to resources and social capital will lead people to regard you as having greater power and influence as well, which, given the social dynamic of organizations, is tantamount to an actual increase in your power and influence at work.

The importance of perceptions to reputation makes it essential to be aware of and carefully orchestrate work behavior and actions so that they transmit the kind of image you want. Reputation is not simply about impression management, of course—you still have to come through and perform effectively. However, individuals with good reputations for being influential and getting things done typically will have no problem building social capital, and that, along with their political skill, should make continued effective performance much easier to accomplish in the future.

Oprah Winfrey is a classic example of the way reputation and influence work reciprocally to enhance each other. Her story is one of unrelenting determination, from her humble beginnings in Mississippi to her current billionaire status. Some consider Oprah lucky—but she herself says you make your own breaks and that luck is simply preparation meeting opportunity (Garson, 2004). *Time* named her one of the hundred most influential people of the twentieth century. Her influence extends across the publishing industry through her famous on-air book club as well as her Angel Network, where in 2000 she began presenting $100,000 "Use Your Life" awards to people who improve the lives of others. Further, she initiated the National Child Protection Act in 1991 and testified before the U.S. Senate Judiciary Committee to develop a national database of convicted child abusers. President Clinton signed the "Oprah Bill" into law in 1993. These are but a few examples of her influence across America and the world. However, her influence would not be nearly as vast if it were not for her reputation as someone who seeks the truth and is empathetic, honest, smart, and loving. Her television personality is engaging and she manages to carry this engaging image wherever she goes. Oprah works hard to maintain her reputation and uses it to make a positive difference in the lives of others.

Conclusion

How much are people concerned about their reputations? Just pick up the newspaper almost any day and you will read about reputational disasters: the succession of famous athletes charged with steroid abuse, the executives of Enron, WorldCom, and Tyco, and many more whose friends and followers desperately urge them to "Say it ain't so!"

It will be interesting to see if the reputations of some of these people, and the human, political, and social capital that form those reputations, will influence the final consequences of their actions. Reputations can sometimes be rebuilt, but trust once violated and sincerity once found to be false are very difficult to repair.

7

MANAGING JOB STRESS

Why is it that some employees thrive in stressful situations while others break down? Why are some so good at coping with complex and changing environments, work-family conflicts, organizational politics, and interpersonal dimensions of their jobs? Employees face numerous work stressors and job demands, and we believe that political skill is a good part of what makes the difference for those who manage to cope smoothly with everything they face.

What political skill does is give you a feeling of control—whatever happens in the workplace, political skill lets you be confident of influencing others so as to reduce or even eliminate threats. This chapter examines the causes of job stress, why job stress is important to organizations as well as individual employees, and how political skill serves both as a coping mechanism in itself and as a way to capitalize on other coping mechanisms that may be available in the environment.

Causes of Job Stress

Job stress generally refers to physiological and psychological reactions to demands encountered at work. Researchers have referred to these responses as experienced stress, or *strain,* and to the forces that cause the responses as *stressors.* Stressors and the conditions that produce them are tough to identify and manipulate, and people's responses to them vary widely; faced with the same conditions, one person will react with delight and another with depressed withdrawal.

Years of research and numerous studies have identified a wide variety of job and organizational stressors, including long hours, heavy workloads, conflicting or ambiguous demands, fast pace, strict deadlines, job insecurity, interpersonal conflict, shift work, organizational politics (which, when causing stress, tends to reflect a *lack* of political skill), and harsh or controlling supervisory styles. In general, the more stressors present in a workplace, the higher the levels of stress employees report.

The most important factor in determining the stressfulness of any given event, however, is whether the stressor is chronic. Chronic stressors hang on with no sign of ending: long-term unemployment, for example, or the need to care for a parent with Alzheimer's. And the reaction to such stressors is not just psychological; people exposed to chronic stressors often lose their immune function and may succumb to a variety of physical ailments.

Many people assume that stress is an inevitable part of life, something to be suffered through rather than something to think about and manage. Indeed, a classic response to complaints about any job is, "That's why they call it *work,* isn't it?" In fact, stress is both possible and desirable to control, and both organizations and the people within them are better off when it is kept to a reasonable level and dealt with constructively.

Consequences of Job Stress

Job stress can do a lot of harm. In the past twenty years, many studies have examined the relationship between job stress and a host of physical and mental ailments. Stress-related concerns include mood and sleep disturbances, upset stomach and headaches, and conflict with family and friends. These symptoms of stress are relatively easy to see, but exposure to chronic stressors can also lead to illnesses that take a long time to develop, such as cardiovascular disease, musculoskeletal disorders, and psychological disorders. Four of the most toxic organizational stressors are ambiguous and changing organizational environments, work-family conflict, organizational politics, and poor interpersonal relationships with colleagues and supervisors. In each case, a lack of political skill is a contributing or even causative factor.

Ambiguity and Change in Organizations

To be competitive these days, organizations must be flexible and adaptable—not merely accepting change but embracing it. Tom Peters (1987) argued that winning companies will be those that constantly change and adapt, that see chaos and ambiguity as market opportunities—and his observation only seems more acute today. Large-scale changes in organizations through restructuring and redesign, business process reengineering, technology adoption, and mergers and acquisitions have been undertaken with the explicit purpose of increasing organizations' chances for survival and success in turbulent environments.

All this change has increased the stress on employees at all levels, and particularly on managers. Organizations now have more flexible structures that are flatter and more rectangular (instead of pyramidal) in shape, and they have diffused and vested more power and authority in those who interface directly with customers and the external environment. Collectively, changes in the internal and external environments of organizations can be expected to increase stress among employees—especially those who had adapted themselves to the traditional bureaucratic structure. As the traditional organization grows less viable and the new flatter structures demand more coordination and decision making at lower levels, political skill—the ability to influence and interact well with other employees as well as outside constituents such as customers—is ever more critical for success.

Work-Family Conflict

The premise of much of the research throughout the past decade is that work-family conflict represents two distinct forms of interrole conflict: work interference with family on one hand and family interference with work on the other. Work-family conflict arises when the demands of being in one domain are incompatible with the demands of being in the other domain. Research has demonstrated that both of these types of conflict can have deleterious effects on work and family outcomes—job dissatisfaction, mental and physical health problems, and poor quality of life.

Work-family conflict is a stressor for both sexes, but it is particularly problematic for working women, who generally devote more hours than men to dealing with the demands of the family. It is more acceptable for men to trade off work for family; women often feel they must do it all. Historically, men's family involvement could vary depending on the demands at work, while the family demands on women tended to be constant and independent of the influence of work. To the extent that the recognition of this inequity changes the attitudes and behavior of both men and women, men's stress levels can be expected to increase somewhat. Women's stress levels probably won't decrease correspondingly in the foreseeable future, however, because there will be more stress to go around—the ever-growing population in and near the oldest age category will put more people of working age into the position of sandwich caregiving, responsible for both parents and children.

Demanding roles, however, do not necessarily lead to experienced stress—some people cope with jobs and families quite well. Political skill seems to be an effective buffer, if only because it helps you realize *when* it is acceptable to say no, as well as *how* to say no.

Organizational Politics

Organizational politics refers to behaviors that are not formally sanctioned by the organization and that produce conflict and disharmony in the work environment by pitting individuals against one another or against the organization. Dealing with organizational politics has been identified as a key and even vital characteristic of effective managers (Kelly & Kaplan, 1993).

It is clear that managers work in highly political contexts as they address competing interests, deal with scarce resources, and try to satisfy multiple stakeholders in efforts to enhance the organization's reputation and success. Unfortunately, not all managers are equally adept and skilled at politics and thus may find the business environment threatening and stressful because of the demand for abilities they lack.

For an example of poor political skill at the highest levels, take a look at "Chainsaw" Al Dunlap. After turning around American Can, Lily-Tulip, Crown Zellerbach, and Scott Paper, Dunlap failed miserably in his attempt to rescue Sunbeam and was fired by the board of directors. His termination was triggered by the discovery that he had tried to disguise a string of serious quarterly losses, and his defenses were weak because his loud, gruff, and demeaning style had alienated the people around him he needed to be successful. Richard L. Boynton, president of the household products division of Sunbeam, described the first series of meetings Dunlap had with his senior staff in unprepossessing terms. He said it was like a dog barking at you for hours. He said Dunlap yelled, ranted, and raved, and was condescending, belligerent, and disrespectful (Byrne, 1999).

Dunlap's approach was to intimidate those around him by telling them in a loud voice over and over again that they were responsible for the failures at Sunbeam. He placed blame on individuals in front of others, threatening to fire them, and in fact did fire a large number of senior executives. Given the stressful organizational environment, some (including many of the most talented) simply left Sunbeam of their own accord. David Fanin, Sunbeam's general counsel, told the board of directors that he could not work for Dunlap another day. The day-to-day atmosphere at the company had really deteriorated and Dunlap was no longer in touch with the business and what was going on at the company. He wasn't talking to people. He had cut himself off (Byrne, 1999). And when he needed help, it wasn't there.

Interpersonal Relationships

Studies of job stress generally identify interpersonal relations as key culprits. Not surprisingly, disruptive and stressful relationships are related to ill health, job dissatisfaction, and absenteeism and turnover.

Even top management positions are far from immune to this sort of stress. Much of the work of management involves interactions with others, and that makes the ability to deal effectively with people with a wide variety of backgrounds, styles, and personalities indispensable for managers—and it makes any weakness in this area a key source of stress. If managers have political skill, they are less likely to experience stress from the interactions required in their jobs.

Which isn't to say that skilled managers never run into stressful interactions, of course. Having and using political skill does not necessarily mean everyone is happy for you. For example, T. K. Wetherell, president of Florida State University (FSU) and former Speaker of the House in Florida, was successful in securing additional funds in 2004 from the state for FSU—largely due to his political savvy. However, Governor Jeb Bush publicly criticized Wetherell for obtaining additional funds for FSU, at the expense of other programs that presumably needed funding, and subsequently chose to veto $17.5 million in FSU construction projects. "I've never been criticized before for being too successful. The board of trustees hired me to find money. I found money. We just worked the system however you work it," Wetherell told the *Tallahassee Democrat* (June 24, 2004, pp. 1A, 2A). Despite the possibility of this sort of setback, however, it's safe to say that most people would prefer the stress of excessive success to that of incomprehensible conflict.

Ways of Coping with Job Stress

Stress may be inevitable, but it need not be overwhelming. Political skill can enhance the effectiveness of coping mechanisms proffered by organizations as well as those developed by individuals.

Organizational Efforts

The evidence that stress impairs performance has become clear enough to persuade many leaders that it makes hard economic sense to help employees cope. Organizational strategies such as job rotation, mandatory breaks and vacations, and a variety of wellness programs, ergonomic adjustments, task and workplace redesign, increased staffing, and role clarification have shown some measure of success in reducing stress levels. In addition, a growing number of organizations have adopted family-supportive programs such as flexible work hours.

Results of these programs often fall far short of their proponents' hopes, however, because people don't take advantage of them. One problem is that permission to have an alternative work arrangement is often based on the manager's personal experiences and beliefs, and the managers tend to lag behind. Research has shown that when employees believe their managers support flexible work schedules, they report lower levels of work-family conflict and psychological and physiological strain (Thomas &

Ganster, 1995). However, whether or not a given manager actually supports such programs, some employees simply don't trust the company, or one another, enough to risk signing up. The quality of the relationship employees have with their supervisors, co-workers, and subordinates strongly affects both the amount of stress they perceive in the workplace and the measures they are willing to take to reduce it.

Political skill does a great deal to ensure good relationships with colleagues at work, which in itself reduces stress. In addition, both managers' reluctance to support flexible work policies and other company measures to reduce employee stress and employees' reluctance to confront their managers over access to such programs can reflect deficiencies in political skill.

Individual Coping

People differ as to their perceptions of and reactions to job stressors, as well as in the way they cope with job stress. Some respond to stress better than others; some try to avoid it (either by fleeing the situation or by damping down their response in an effort to stop feeling the stress), while others try to either adapt themselves to the situation or adapt it to their preferences. Avoidance is most likely when people see no way to adjust anything so as to ease the strain. Unfortunately, short of leaving the job entirely—which also involves stresses—avoidance rarely does much to improve the situation in the long run.

Political Skill as a Coping Mechanism

The near future offers little hope for those low in political skill. Stress will continue to increase as competition intensifies, labor market conditions create a scarcity of talent in some fields and a glut in others, technology continues to change in rapid and unpredictable ways, and the degree of accountability at all levels of organizations increases. Research suggests that many work environments are becoming increasingly noxious, pushing illnesses related to the physical and mental effects of stress to an all-time high ("Worker stress, health reaching critical point," 1999).

How do employees cope with increased work stressors and experienced strain? Purely individual approaches such as exercise, relaxation techniques, vacations, and so on can help for a while, but the stress always returns. In contrast, political skill can serve as an enduring antidote to the potentially devastating consequences to health and well-being of stressful work environments. It provides a protective mechanism that allows people to not simply withstand but even flourish in intensely stressful environments.

Political Skill as an Antidote to Stress

Employees high in political skill actively seek out and relish the dynamics of interpersonal interaction. The sense of control they feel contributes to the calm confidence that goes along with the high predictability of success. Indeed, such employees welcome the opportunity to demonstrate their political skill so much that their job tension and stress recede with increasing opportunities to work with others.

We know a senior consultant in a large, well-known consulting firm who thrives on conflict. Her job involves resolving disputes between clients and the consulting firm regarding interpretations and implementation of consultant recommendations. Many people hate the idea of this sort of negotiation and avoid it whenever they can—and suffer when they can't. This consultant loves it, and she is almost always successful in resolving the issues involved so that both the client and the consulting firm are happy and final billing problems are avoided. She sees these situations as an opportunity to demonstrate her unique competence in the firm.

The idea that managers need political skill is nothing new, of course; but what is new is our observation that the effective use of political skill can be a way to reduce job stress and thereby improve executive health. For one thing, simply having political skill can directly reduce the effects of organizational stressors. Research has found that concerns about self-presentation and managing impressions can lead to social anxiety with potential health risks (Leary, 1995). Employees high in political skill are free of such concerns; confident of their ability to control images, impressions, and interactions at work, they are less likely to perceive their situation as stressful. Further, when employees do not perceive their organizational situation to be stressful, they are less likely to experience psychological and physiological strain.

In addition, political skill serves as a buffer between perceived stressors and strain: even when employees do perceive their organization as stressful, they can use their political skill as a coping mechanism to reduce negative consequences. We have found that political skill reduced both physiological and psychological strain in employees who were under chronic stress. That study (reported in Perrewé et al., 2004) examined chronic role conflict in organizations (the perception of conflicting objectives and demands) and, not surprisingly, found a number of psychological and physiological ailments associated with it. Compared to subjects with low political skill, those with high political skill experienced lower heart rates and blood pressure and had fewer complaints about physical ailments and anxiety.

Implications of Political Skill

Several issues are critical to political skill as an antidote to stress on the job. First, those high in political skill have good reason to believe—based on repeated experience—that they can control the processes and outcomes of interactions with others. Thus, political skill creates feelings of success, accomplishment, and confidence, and such feelings tend to enhance physical as well as mental health. Second, employees with strong political skill will view interpersonal interactions as opportunities rather than as threats, so the same environment that seems stressful to the unskilled is merely invigorating to the skillful.

How might political skill benefit employees in terms of the specific causes of stress we have set forth here? Organizational ambiguity, unclear roles, and turbulence are all aspects of the interpersonal context—getting things done in this context always requires working with and through other people—and political skill makes them all seem more manageable.

Accountability is another stressor shown to place demands on employees. The politically skilled employee will be less threatened by the need to manage multiple and divergent constituencies and interpersonal relationships. Political skill both enhances the results you're accountable for and makes it easier to recover from shortfalls or divert the consequences to another target. Even in contexts such as stockholder meetings where the executive may serve as a lightning rod, the ability to inspire trust and confidence may well serve to transfer the distress to other circumstances or even to the more vocal detractors.

We know a senior executive in a high-tech defense company who enjoys dealing with stockholder groups, civic organizations, and the press. Even though many executives find dealing with these groups stressful, he does not. He is a retired Air Force general with extensive overseas experience in intelligence. His quick wit and strong analytical thinking—combined with some unusual skills (for example, he speaks fluent Chinese and sings opera)—allow him to charm even the most hostile audience. He views each battle with potentially hostile stockholders or the press as a unique opportunity to demonstrate his political skill.

The implications for political skill regarding organizational politics and interpersonal relationships as stressors are straightforward. The ability to work comfortably in a political environment and define its dimensions as interpersonal suggests a natural fit between the politically skilled person and executive-level work. Rather than regarding the political and interpersonal aspects of the job as threatening, hard to understand, and uncontrollable, the skilled employee is apt to recognize that they are essential to the job and that they provide a chance to shine.

That is, situations that call for political skill are seen as opportunities by those who are adept at using that skill. Those not so adept experience frustration, try other methods such as the intimidation used by Al Dunlap, or just ignore the situation. This causes personal stress and creates stress among employees and throughout the organization. The proper use of political skill has the opposite effect: it reduces stress not only for the users themselves but also for those around them, thus creating a healthier organization.

Organizational Benefits

The organization as a whole stands to reap great rewards if the employees are better able to communicate, engage in interpersonal interactions, cope with accountabilities, operate in a turbulent environment, and be flexible. As a result, formal efforts to improve political skill have implications beyond feel-good employee benefits. The organization enjoys better success, encounters fewer causes of anxiety, and enjoys better relationships with customers, suppliers, and potential allies in the market. Its whole operation becomes more effective, because every detail, from external negotiations to the shared work of teams and offices, runs more smoothly on a base of political skill.

Managing and coping with accountabilities has external as well as internal implications. Many organizations suffer from public image or regulatory compliance problems that can be minimized or mitigated by the application of political skill.

A CASE IN POINT: SEPTEMBER 11, 2001

Organizations are widely viewed as political arenas and it is long past time for us to seriously consider the repertoire of skills that contribute to a healthy and successful work environment. But political skill and leadership operate in a much broader spectrum—although the focus of this book is on organizations, the political skill and leadership portrayed by Mayor Giuliani during the 9/11 terrorist attacks is an important example of how political skill can reduce experienced stress not only for the one applying the skill but for everyone around.

Clearly, the 9/11 attack in New York is an extreme example of stress. Nonetheless, Mayor Rudolph Giuliani deserves a tremendous amount of credit for his political skill and leadership during this horrific time. As the Twin Towers collapsed, Giuliani quickly devised a plan of action. "I divided my mission into three parts: First, I had to communicate with the public to do whatever I could to calm people down and contribute to an orderly and safe evacuation. Second, I wanted to prepare for the injured. . . . Third, I was considering 'What will happen next?' . . . I tried to get inside the heads of the terrorists. What were they going to attack next?" (Giuliani, 2002, pp. 16–17).

Although he couldn't sleep that night because of his anxiety and sorrow, he knew his leadership was needed. The next day, he called the usual early morning meeting of his deputies and commissioners—a practice he'd followed virtually every day since 1981. "The importance of the 'morning meeting' cannot be overstated. I consider it the cornerstone to efficient functioning within a system, especially a complex one." The main purpose of the morning meeting was to "get control of the day" (p. 29). "The point was not to get a head start on the task at hand, but to set a tone—for myself and for those who looked to me for leadership" (p. 37).

All this came into play after the attack. Giuliani demonstrated leadership skills by making sure he reduced ambiguity and set clear goals in the morning meeting. The political skill came in when he focused on setting a tone for everyone. He worked hard to remain calm and he was able to inspire others to trust him and to follow his orders. Not only did his political skill help him neutralize his experienced stress, it helped him reduce the experienced stress of others. Because others trusted him, they followed his directives and were calmer.

People with good political skill are able to get those around them to work as a team. "Looking back, I believe that the skill I developed better than any other was surrounding myself with great people," Giuliani (2002) writes. "The group in place on September 11th proved to be exceptionally strong—especially since so much of what we had to do in the light of the disaster had no precedent" (p. 98). After the terrorist attacks, Mayor Giuliani demonstrated leadership, but, more important, he was able to use his political skill to inspire others to trust his judgment and to carry out their duties—even in the face of tremendous uncertainty, sorrow, and stress.

Conclusion

For many reasons, job stress is increasing in organizations, and, indeed, stress at work has become a monumental health problem. Therefore, we not only need to identify causes of stress in the workplace, we also need to explore and try to understand ways people can cope with stress effectively. Political skill clearly plays a role in this process, serving as an antidote to the dysfunctional strain effects that can harm people in work organizations. Obviously, stress can affect people at all levels and in all types of jobs, but it is a significant problem for top executives and leaders, who are under ever-increasing scrutiny. Such individuals particularly can realize the benefits of being politically skilled, and the next chapter examines how political skill serves to increase the effectiveness of leaders.

8

Building Leadership and Team Performance

The concept of leadership has generated great interest for centuries, much of it devoted to a search for the characteristics of effective leaders. Even today, it is rare to pick up a newspaper or magazine and not read about leaders—presidents, military officers, corporate CEOs, coaches. And despite the variety of arenas where leadership manifests, most people seem to believe that the characteristics of effective leaders are constant—that the same qualities make for an effective five-star general, CEO of a major corporation in any line of business, or any other organization head.

But that's about where agreement ends. What qualities, what specific set of characteristics, really distinguishes the most effective leaders—remains debatable.

We won't attempt a complete definition here, but we believe that political skill must be high on any useful list, because that is what makes it possible for a leader to effect critical and needed change. In this chapter, we discuss how political skill plays a central role in the leadership process, whether you are influencing another individual, leading a multibillion-dollar corporation, or coaching a football team.

The Main Ingredient in the Leadership Recipe

One constant element among definitions of leadership is influence: leaders define and interpret events, inspire, motivate,
orchestrate, and coach as needed to achieve their goals. As
President Harry Truman once said: "A leader . . . has the ability to
get other people to do what they don't want to do and like it"
(quoted in Matthews, 1988, p. 195).

If leadership is an influence process, then to be effective at it,
you need at least two basic qualities. You need *political will,* that is,
the desire, motivation, or propensity to exercise influence (Mintzberg,
1983). You also need *political skill,* the style and savvy to make the
influence successful, which is a different matter entirely and crucial if you want to lead. Without the will to lead, political skill is an
underutilized resource, smoothing your path in small ways. But
without the skill to exercise influence effectively, political will is
only an endless source of difficulty and disruption.

Political Skill and the Obscure
Nature of Leader Style

Leader style is the manner in which leaders express particular
behaviors, the way they do what they do that makes others perceive them as leaders and defer to them. Indeed, it has been suggested that the effectiveness of leaders is ultimately judged on the
basis of their style (Bolman & Deal, 1991), and that it is as much
a matter of how they say things as of what they say (Gardner &
Avolio, 1998). So, leader style is another concept that has been
discussed for years—again with no satisfactory consensus. The
only conclusion reached by experts after years of examining
leader style is that no one really knows exactly what it is or how it
might affect leadership (House & Aditya, 1997).

We suggest that leader style is basically encompassed in the
concept of political skill. Leader style involves the execution of

behavior that contributes to effectiveness, and so does political skill. But political skill also encompasses the necessary preconditions for effective behavior: the sound reading of a situation and astute understanding of what behavior is required—and of how to use that behavior to convey sincerity and concern for the common good. In addition, the networking component of political skill generates the social capital that is vital for success in group undertakings.

Leader Social Capital

Social capital is built by developing networks and their associated social connections and ties, which gives you access to resources you can use to advance your own aims. (This is not as manipulative as it sounds when stated so baldly, of course, as you also make yourself available for others to use. In general, the service is mutual; either simultaneously or over the long haul, everyone in a social network benefits.) Politically skilled leaders accumulate extensive stores of social capital through their ability to embed themselves in diverse networks of talented and influential people. In one study, Fred Luthans and his associates (1988) identified networking as the activity successful managers engaged in most frequently, and it involved the use of political skill to gain competitive advantage.

The alliances, coalitions, and friendship networks leaders build inside and outside the organization contribute to a favorable reputation and significant positioning within the network, which allows for greater access to information, greater influence, and greater capacity to generate trust and cooperation. Politically skilled leaders are adept at the use of favors to inspire personal obligation and commitment from those around them. This all greatly increases their power and influence.

Harry Truman's definition—getting people to like doing what they don't want to do—is an appropriate way to think about leadership.

It conjures up images of inspiration, motivation, coaching, and orchestration and facilitation of the effort of others to exercise influence in ways that maximize goal accomplishment. These behaviors reflect the style of politically skilled leaders. Interestingly, over the years, the question we have heard most often from managers in organizations (either in consulting projects or in seminars and classes) is, "How do you motivate employees?"

This perennial question brings to mind a variety of possible answers that relate to specific views on leadership. For some, motivating employees involves being very directive and almost dragging them in the right direction. For others, it involves reinforcing desired behaviors with rewards and extinguishing undesired behaviors by withholding rewards or applying sanctions and punishments. What these two views have in common is that they position the leader as making employees do things they really don't want to do.

However, Truman's mark of good leadership—to get people to do something they don't want to do *and to feel good about doing it*— seems to call for a different view. So, then, back to the question about how leaders motivate their people. Well, our best answer is—you don't. You can't do it by dragging or luring them along; but you can create the conditions and circumstances whereby they will motivate themselves. How can you accomplish this? It takes that subtle but powerful quality we call political skill.

OK, so leader style is encompassed in political skill, but exactly how does it play out in terms of leaders' efforts to use this style or political skill on others? In the next sections, we examine how politically skilled leaders make strategic use of rhetoric, language, and communication to accomplish their goals.

Political Skill and the Communication of Leadership

Leadership often involves defining and interpreting events for others. That makes the act of leadership, and even the very way we come to identify people as leaders, intertwine intricately with language, rhetoric, symbolism, and nonverbal communication, all of which are designed to convey certain images.

Louis Pondy (1978) captured a lot of truth when he called leadership a "language game"—an activity where meanings, not words, reflect what is being communicated. For purposes of discussion, we separate leadership as communication into the three separate categories of language and rhetoric, symbolic behavior, and nonverbal behavior and strategic emotion communication. However, the influence process inherent in leadership is something that is brought to life by a strategic integration of all three.

Language and Rhetoric

Verbal language represents the most common way we communicate with others in organizations and in everyday life and thus represents a strong basis of influence. The term *rhetoric* sums up both the process itself and the ambiguity people feel toward its deliberate use, as it denotes the effective use of words to persuade or influence others but further suggests an element of artificial eloquence and showy elaboration in the effort. Research in leadership has depicted charismatic leaders as strategically employing rhetoric to manage impressions and influence, motivate, and persuade others (Gardner & Avolio, 1998).

Information that materializes through debate, conversation, and verbal interaction forms the basis for much of how people perceive their world, which makes language a potent form of social influence (Pfeffer, 1992). Furthermore, it is through language that people experience the political realities of organizations, and this happens largely through the efforts of leaders to interpret what goes on in the organization and make it meaningful—which is a major aspect of political skill.

Strategic communication—that is, interaction designed to accomplish specific goals and objectives—often deliberately employs ambiguity and confusion rather than clarity. Counterintuitive though it may seem, strategic ambiguity in communication can be a way to manage meaning and thereby exercise influence by capitalizing on lack of agreement concerning the meaning of activities and events in the organization. It is a matter of stock humor that politicians and top managers use intentional equivocation and vagueness in strategic efforts to protect their positions—but they do it in real life, too, and it often works—partly as a result of their political skill, and partly as a result of their followers' lack of skill.

It seems that communication is used strategically to accomplish a variety of goals in organizations, only one of which may be clarity or authenticity. Managers generally perceive one of their key roles as providing clarity, definition, and direction for employees, and this role is diminished if things are too clear. Therefore, in a situation where goals, procedures, and so forth are clear, managers with low to moderate political skill might actively engineer increased ambiguity so they could then provide solutions to clarify it. Managers with greater political skill, in contrast, might instead negotiate new roles that took advantage of existing clarity to provide hitherto unfeasible benefits to the organization (Buckman, 2004).

Symbolic Behavior

Communication in organizations does far more than impart knowledge and information. It can be symbolic, intended to convey meanings and exercise influence. *Symbolic behavior* is concerned with how individuals create or enact their environments by creating shared meanings and understandings (Russ, 1991). Jeffrey Pfeffer points out that it "operates fundamentally on the principle of illusion, in that using political language, settings, and ceremonies effectively elicits powerful emotions in people, and these emotions interfere with or becloud rational analysis" (1992, p. 279).

Symbolic behavior is an important part of how reputations are created and maintained, and business leaders and politicians alike work hard at manipulating symbols to create the perception that they are powerful. Their resulting power is based less on reality than on appearance—but perception is reality in many cases, especially where suggestions and implied desires can be taken as commands. Symbolic communication is thus probably most effective in ambiguous working environments, which put most emphasis on the leaders' interpretations of events.

Through language, communication, and symbolic behavior, managers can switch the focus of their performance evaluation from outcomes to behaviors or simply render outcomes and behaviors indistinguishable. George Gallup once said, "People tend to judge a man by his goals, by what he's trying to do, and not necessarily by what he accomplishes or by how well he succeeds" (quoted in Edelman, 1964, p. 78). If this is so, then leaders can orchestrate situations to their advantage through the strategic use of symbolism, language, and rhetoric. This led Jeffrey Pfeffer to conclude, "Political language is often effective because people are judged by their intent, by the symbolism of what they are seeking to accomplish, rather than by the reality of what they are doing" (1992, p. 288).

Nonverbal Communication and Strategic Emotion

In addition to what you say, the way you say it—your facial expressions, nonverbal behavior, and the emotions you choose to demonstrate—can represent important and influential mechanisms of influence. Of the several processes that constitute strategic nonverbal influence, impression management is the most relevant, and nonverbal behavior plays a key role in forming impressions. Politically skilled individuals are the most successful at the effective execution of nonverbal communication because they present it in the most genuine and convincing manner.

The use of expressed emotion as a source of strategic influence is an important part of everyday life, particularly so on the job. You laugh at the boss's jokes whether or not you find them amusing; you sometimes feign anger with a co-worker or sadness with a subordinate to strategically convey a certain image that will influence the reactions you receive. When things go wrong, you might act more distressed than you feel—even crying if it would be socially acceptable for you to do so—to divert wrath, thus making a strategic display of emotion designed to temper the response.

The content of displayed emotion is apparent in language, gestures, facial expressions, and tones of voice—displays Erving Goffman (1959) summed up as "control moves." The use of emotion to control is important, but it depends on *displayed* emotions. These are not necessarily the same as *experienced* emotions, and it is often counterproductive to allow genuine feelings to show. If your boss makes a comment that makes you angry, displaying anger openly based on what you are experiencing might conceivably cut through the problem and clear the air—but chances are it will only make things worse. Politically skilled individuals understand their emotions and express them in constructive ways.

Some jobs (airline flight attendant, for example) have formal rules that specify the proper emotions to express. It is simply part of the job to treat passengers in a friendly, smiling manner, and the flight attendant need not experience friendship to express good cheer. Although most workplaces don't have such explicit rules, most develop conventions as to when and to what extent which emotions can or should be displayed.

Politically skilled individuals are able to control their emotional displays effectively and convincingly, and they have the ability to express emotions over an extended period of time, reflecting what Arlie Hochschild (1983) calls "emotional stamina." Some leaders know just how and when to display emotion strategically, perhaps to show a softer side, such as when discussing a tragic event.

For example, as president, Bill Clinton was a master at the combination of rhetoric, nonverbal behavior, and strategic emotion to convey points he wished to make forcefully and above all convincingly. He is a living illustration of the relationship between political skill and communication. His supporters and detractors alike marveled at his ability to position himself in ways that ensured success and allowed him to emerge from the depths of adversity unscathed. Televised speeches, interviews, and press conferences constantly showed Clinton's strategic use of pauses for effect, nonverbal behavior, and emotion control to convey powerful and believable images.

Clinton accomplished his reputational sleight of hand with his amazing level of political skill, and by using his ability to interpret and reinterpret reality, treating events as mere "text"—"subject to infinite interpretations and linguistic manipulation—but never to definitive judgment" (Morrow, 1998, p. 29). Indeed, this reinforces the importance of spin, where reality is nonexistent, interpretations are manipulated through image management, and, as Tom Peters once said, "there's no such thing as steak, sad to say, just the sizzle" (quoted in Kanter & Mirvis, 1989, p. 130).

Applying Spin

Language, rhetoric, symbolic behavior, nonverbal communication, and the calculated demonstration of emotion can all help you exert social influence toward the people around you, whether an individual or a group. Where do you learn such behavior? Given the focus on rhetoric and symbolism through various communication media as characterizing what leaders do, perhaps business schools and in-house training departments should reconsider the most appropriate types of training to prepare future managers to fulfill their various roles. Because so much of managerial and leadership work focuses on symbols, images, and interpretation, we agree with Karl Weick's assessment: the "appropriate role for the manager may be evangelist rather than accountant" (1979, p. 42). Jeffrey Pfeffer has argued along the same lines: "The importance of ceremonies and language in the development and use of power has sometimes led me to recommend acting, literature, or English classes to aspiring managerial leaders" (1992, pp. 295–296).

If leaders can be compared to stage and screen actors, it should be no surprise that acting and drama classes seem to be catching on as management and leadership development, as we discussed in Chapter 3. A number of business schools seem to be taking stock of such demands on managers, offering courses in dealing with the media as useful vehicles for managing your career and enhancing the image of your company (Deutsch, 1990).

Indeed, much time and attention is devoted to the "construction and manipulation of the image of the leader," by acting coaches, speech writers, and media advisers (Gardner, 1995, p. 60). Of course, the real key is not to just learn to *play* the role, however convincingly, but to *become* the person in the role, which will contribute to increased perceptions of authenticity; such authenticity is best carried out by people high in political skill.

Charisma and Political Skill

The characteristic we see associated with leadership probably more than any other is *charisma,* that special quality that tends to inspire people to follow a vision or course of action. Nonetheless, until a couple of decades ago, the leaders of large corporations were routinely selected on the basis of their performance track record, as though charisma either was unimportant or implied by their track record in lower management positions. That approach no longer works. Rakesh Khurana, who conducted one of the largest studies of CEO selection ever made, confirms that you can't just be a "competent manager" today and be selected to run a Fortune 500 company; you must be seen as a "charismatic leader" (2002, p. 71). He argues that this change in selection trend can be dated to 1979, when Lee Iacocca took over the Chrysler Corporation and orchestrated its amazing turnaround, taking the corporation from ashes to success. In the process, he catapulted himself into celebrity status. (We briefly profiled Iacocca in Chapter 6.) Indeed, as Khurana aptly notes, "CEOs have become the equivalent of rock stars" (p. 251), and, promoted aggressively by the media, they regularly grace the covers of major magazines.

The recent scandals at corporations such as Enron, WorldCom, and Tyco, and the top executives involved, may be driven by creatures created, at least partially, by the national media.

Leader charisma has, indeed, been a topic of intense interest. However, if the ability to inspire people to action generally is what we mean by charisma, then it would seem to be encompassed in political skill. That is, politically skilled leaders are effective because they astutely read contexts and adjust, adapt, and calibrate their behavior to create the desired image, use their social capital to further reinforce their image, and do all this in a sincere, authentic, and convincing way.

Thus viewed, charisma becomes simply part of the competency set we call political skill. We agree with the suggestion that leaders engage in active efforts to manage impressions of their charisma (Gardner & Avolio, 1998), and we maintain that it is political skill that allows such efforts to succeed.

Political Skill and Top Executives

As we noted at the outset, organizations are political arenas. The practice of politics at work is a fact of life, and it only increases as you go up the corporate hierarchy. For top executives, political skill is not just beneficial for success and effectiveness, it is essential.

Much of what top executives do is symbolic in nature—and thus susceptible to image creation and manipulation. This observation is far from new; as Cyril Sofer pointed out, "The would-be successful executive learns when to simulate enthusiasm, compassion, interest, concern, modesty, confidence, and mastery, when to smile, with whom to laugh, and how intimate to be with others. If the operation succeeds, he will have fabricated a personality in harmony with his environment" (1970, p. 61). As Robert Jackall puts it, successful managers "learn to wear all the right masks, learn all the right vocabularies of discourse, get to know all the right people, and cultivate the subtleties of the art of self-promotion" (1988, p. 74). That is, managers and executives must consciously manage the image they project, and do so to perfection, with political skill. The social astuteness and interpersonal influence facets of political skill play key roles here, and, of course, none of this works if not done convincingly, that is, in an apparently sincere and genuine way.

And networking ability also is critical to managerial effectiveness. In fact, Fred Luthans and his associates (1988) found that effective managers spend nearly half their time on networking activities, much more than they devote to what would be considered traditional managerial activities. Leadership involves goal accomplishment with and through others, and the social capital that accrues to those with political skill is what makes it possible for leaders to be effective—thus further illustrating the critical role such skill plays in organizational life.

Accountability and Reputation

Political skill, accountability, trust, and reputation come together to enhance leader effectiveness. In Chapter 6, we discussed the role of political skill in the development and maintenance of reputations, and the same observations apply here to leadership because of the immense role reputation plays in leaders' ability to be effective.

That is, political skill influences the formation of leader reputation and causes others to trust leaders more; also, those with greater trust tend to give leaders more leeway. So politically skilled leaders have the freedom to go beyond normal restrictions on behavior because their people expect them to do only things that benefit them and the organization. Unfortunately, that works only as long as it works; when the expectations are based on reality and leaders do engage only in beneficial behaviors, all is well, but leaders sometimes buy into the view that anything they do is by definition right. At that point, they easily slip into behaviors that help themselves but not the organization.

In fact, this is one way we can make sense of the corporate scandals at Enron, WorldCom, and Tyco in recent years. For example, was Tyco CEO Dennis Kozlowski given more leeway to do what he wanted and held less accountable for the results because of his reputation, political skill, and the trust that they produced? It certainly seems so. He apparently felt no duty to his employer when he looted Tyco for millions of dollars in personal vacations, paintings, furnishings, and more.

Consider also the case of football coach Mike Price. Based on his winning record, Price was hired as head coach at the University of Alabama—which had been one of the most prestigious coaching jobs in the country since legendary coach Paul "Bear" Bryant built the team into a perennial national powerhouse. But Price was fired before he ever coached a game at Alabama. His personal indiscretions before the season began reflected the behavior of someone who let his celebrity status go to his head; he seemed to believe he was not accountable for his actions. Maybe he thought he was going to be accountable only for how many games he won and not for his behavior off the field, even though he was a highly visible representative of the university. He may have thought of himself as following Bryant, who'd been cut a lot of slack concerning off-field behavior precisely because he did win a lot of football games—but Price hadn't won anything for Alabama yet, and he was operating in a social climate that had changed since Bryant's day.

To depict reputation simply we can say it includes two components: performance and integrity. Today, both are needed, whereas years ago, if leaders were very successful at producing the results they were measured by (profitability for executives, won-lost record for coaches, and the like), they could behave in just about any way they wanted, and it was tolerated or even hushed up. Those leaders didn't have to be discreet, they just needed to post high performance records. High status and a good reputation still entice some leaders to engage in unethical, immoral, or illegal behavior, but nowadays leaders with true political skill are too astute to fall into the celebrity trap.

Trust

Trust is another component of political skill that helps leaders be viewed favorably, even in cases where they fall short of a goal or demonstrate questionable behavior. Politically skilled leaders tend to engender trust, so if they do something wrong, people's initial reaction is to attribute the behavior to failed positive intentions, just bad luck, or someone else's doing. Leaders low in political skill, who might not be trusted or viewed as good people, find the public is quicker to attribute poor performance or questionable behavior to self-serving intentions.

The motives or intentions attributed to behavior affect people's reactions to it. The public might howl for punishment for someone who behaved immorally if they thought the misdeed was intentional but not if they thought it was caused by someone or something else. It is natural to like—as well as trust and believe in—politically skilled people, so when they do something wrong, the first instinct is to look for reasons it was not their fault.

The Martha Stewart case is an interesting one. Although she gained recognition as a television celebrity and a successful businesswoman, Stewart does not appear to have much political skill. It seems clear from public reaction to the prison sentence she received after being found guilty of lying to federal investigators about a 2001 stock trade that people were not sympathetic. They didn't seem to like, trust, or believe in her, and that reaction might have a lot to do with the media posturing Stewart engaged in throughout the legal proceedings, showing little if any remorse and no humility. She seemed to position herself as above the law, unapologetic, and indignant in her claims of innocence.

Political Skill of Elected Officials

Partisan politics has always been an arena for influence, whether it be face-to-face persuasion or coalition or network building designed to muster sufficient support to push through, or block, legislation. Political skill is obviously important in politics, and it may well be the most important characteristic that distinguishes truly effective political leaders. Politicians operate in a world of image creation and management, where there is more interpretation of fact than reality, and their (or their advisers') ability to promote ideas with the proper spin is critical to success or even survival. Thus politics provides an arena not that different from the way influence is exercised in organizations or life in general; political skill is critically important in all these contexts; it is simply more widely recognized among those who compete for office.

For example, what characteristics do people look for in a U.S. president? Obviously, there are about as many answers to this question as there are people to ask, but some interesting similarities appear across media polls. The American public seems to want a president who looks and acts presidential, which includes style, temperament, likability, and authenticity, or at least their appearance.

If candidates are perceived as phony, the public won't like them nor vote for them; if candidates are perceived as charismatic, people tend to like them and will probably vote for them. So liking candidates is important, because then people probably trust them more and have more of a comfort level with them. Politically skilled candidates understand this well and are skillful at managing impressions that lead to favorable outcomes. Because politicians have a reputation for phoniness, the candidates who succeed appear sincere, genuine, and authentic—that is, the what-you-see-is-what-you-get sort of people. This is a key competency of the politically skilled, and it can make the difference in an election.

In *The Presidential Difference: Leadership Style from FDR to George W. Bush* (2004), Fred Greenstein evaluates our recent presidents on the important qualities of organizational capacity, vision, emotional intelligence, public communication, political skill, and cognitive style. Particularly noteworthy for our purposes here are the latter three of these qualities.

Public communication involves leadership capabilities of masterful use of rhetoric, language, and symbolic behavior (as we discussed earlier in this chapter) to convey ideas. Roosevelt,

Kennedy, Reagan, and Clinton were at their best as effective public communicators, according to Greenstein.

Greenstein refers to political skill as the assertive use of power to build support for policies and establish a reputation among others in the political arena for understanding and being able to work the political system to one's advantage. Lyndon Johnson is Greenstein's pick as the master of political skill, with Roosevelt, Reagan, and Clinton also highly developed in this area. Harry Truman is not usually regarded as particularly noteworthy for political skill, but he did seem to perfect the art of persuasion. Greenstein points out that Truman developed "the art of getting along with others," and he quotes Truman as acknowledging that aspect of political skill: "Because of my efforts to get along with my associates I usually was able to get what I wanted" (p. 40).

Greenstein suggested that Roosevelt and Reagan provide excellent examples of how limitations in intelligence, or cognitive style, did not limit their presidential effectiveness, which was carried mostly by their excellent communication ability and political skill. Clinton's political skill was exceptional as well, but he was also known for his high level of intelligence. Newt Gingrich said about Clinton, "He's very smart, he has great personal skills, and he was willing to give away practically anything to survive. In energy level, you could compare him to Theodore Roosevelt. In personal political skills, you would compare him to FDR" ("The Clinton Legacy," 2001, p. 6A).

Political Skill in Higher Education

Increasingly, we see similarities between the arena of partisan and electoral politics and the arena of higher education at the top levels, where the skills and competencies required of university presidents involve more and more political adeptness. What used to get someone placed on the short list by search committees for university president positions was an impeccable set of academic credentials:

a doctorate from a prestigious university followed by a distinguished record of accomplishment as a scholar in that field of study. Such credentials were believed to be necessary (and desirable) because they would command the respect and acceptance of the reputable scholars who served on the faculty of the university in question.

However, in recent years, particularly at public universities that depend on the state legislature for a portion of their budgets, university presidents are spending more of their time in the state capitals lobbying for increased budgets for faculty and staff salaries, adding or improving facilities, and the like. Influence ability, networks, connections, coalition building, and familiarity with the legislative process are real assets that can distinguish effective university presidents.

When Florida State University (FSU) hired Dr. T. K. Wetherell as its new president in 2002, it chose a community college president out of an impressive list of qualified candidates that included the president of Ohio State University and others of similarly high academic credentials. What made the difference? The time Wetherell had spent in the Florida state legislature, where he'd served for several years as the Speaker of the House.

The local newspaper article that reported on the selection noted, "A university president's political skills—knowing where to find the money, which legislators to see about new programs—mean more than academic credentials. . . . Connections were at least equally important in his selection. . . . He has the ability to get people to trust him. . . . Wetherell has a good combination of intelligence, persuasiveness, and toughness. . . . T. K. has a giant reputation" (Cotterell, 2002, pp. 1A, 4A).

In an interview with T. K. Wetherell, we asked him to define political skill. He replied, "I think political skill is getting people to do things they would not normally try to do—get them to believe they can do the work." He added, "I am the weakest link in the chain—everyone else does the hard work. . . . I simply know how to get them to do the work." When asked about leaders he regarded as having political skill, he mentioned both Clinton and Reagan and then said, "I met Bill Clinton five times, and he is both charismatic and brilliant. When one combines charisma with ability, that is a powerful combination. When I spoke with Clinton, even in a room with fifty other people, he always made me feel that I was the most important and interesting person in the room. I met Reagan one time and he had that same presence about him. It's hard to define political skill, but people know it when they see it."

Leadership, Political Skill, and Team Performance

The word *leadership*, of course, raises the implicit question, Leadership of what? Leadership implies team, group, or unit performance.

The changes in organizations noted in Chapter 1 suggest that the role of leaders is changing. A leader, once described as an overseer or gatekeeper, is better described today as a coach or facilitator and a motivator. Instead of ensuring that employees are adhering to rigid, top-down bureaucratic rules, today's successful leaders are eliminating barriers—including structural impediments in the organization—and facilitating and orchestrating the efforts of employees toward collective goals. These changes inherently require managers to possess a different set of skills than their predecessors needed.

Without doubt, effective leaders in organizations, today and in the future, will need to focus their energies toward interpersonal activities such as coaching, coordination, and orchestration. This is especially true in team-based organizational settings, which are becoming more and more prevalent these days, where leader behavior plays a critical role in influencing team performance.

The type of participation that leaders foster among team members makes a big difference in overall performance. Teams with substantive participation (that is, the ones whose leaders relinquish some measure of control to subordinates) generally outperform teams where subordinate input is limited to consultation (Batt & Appelbaum, 1995). Substantive participation means less direct control and new risk for the leader. Because of this, it might be that political skill can be used to constrain autonomous subordinates, and thus it is used as a subtle means of accomplishing influence aimed at goal achievement. This suggests that politically skilled leaders intuitively read their followers and do not exhibit the same style for everyone they lead. Instead, they know to adjust the way they lead to the unique needs and talents of each subordinate. (For more on the topic of leader-member exchange, see Graen & Uhl-Bien, 1995, reflecting some twenty-five years of research by George Graen.)

The relationship between leader political skill and team performance goes beyond the theoretical. For example, in a study of casework leaders in a large state child welfare system, political skill on the part of the leader turned out to be a significant predictor of team performance, measured in terms of placement of children in legally final living arrangements. This relationship held even after controlling for the influences of leader experience, team member experience, average number of team placements, average age of children served, and average caseload of teams (Ahearn, Ferris, Hochwarter, Douglas, & Ammeter, 2004).

Although the casework study was interesting and important, it provided no understanding of just how or why leader political skill influenced team performance. Another study attempted to build on this research and examined the possibility that leader political skill might influence followers by making them feel greater support from the leader and the organization, which in turn would lead to greater trust in the leader and subsequently increased commitment to the organization. The researchers found that leader political skill did lead to followers' perceptions of support, which led to trust, which subsequently affected follower commitment to the organization, all of which was believed to make the followers more attached and productive (Treadway et al., 2004).

As noted, effective leadership is often defined in terms of the performance of the team being led, and politically skilled leaders can facilitate interaction, orchestrate action, inspire effort, and coach followers to perform better as a team. We extend those observations now to coaches who have led successful sports teams and to how they use political skill to increase team performance. We could select any of a number of sports and find successful coaches in each, but because of its tremendous popularity, we focus on college football.

Certainly, college football history is rich in successful coaches, including such legends as Knute Rockne of Notre Dame and Paul "Bear" Bryant of Alabama, as well as famous current coaches such as Joe Paterno of Penn State and Bobby Bowden of Florida State. We do not have the space to devote to an examination of the political skill of each of these men, but we believe that, in Bobby Bowden, we have a wonderful example borne out by his account of his life (2001). Indeed, Bowden is on track to complete his coaching career as the winningest coach in the history of Division I college football. Bobby Bowden has been so successful because he both understands the game of football very well and has excellent political skill.

Just what are the necessary qualities of successful football coaches, and how do those qualities and characteristics get translated into their teams' actual performance? Bobby Bowden seems to possess many of the very same qualities we've described in politically skilled and effective corporate executives, politicians, and presidents. You don't have to spend much time with Bowden to find that he lives by a set of strong principles from which he does not stray. He is self-confident but never arrogant—in fact, he believes strongly in the importance of humility. Also, he is a person of integrity, enthusiasm, and loyalty, and he leads by example.

As Bowden admits, an important part of what he does is to persuade and influence people who play for him, both in the recruitment process and in day-to-day coaching. He has to apply his political skill to ensure team effectiveness. He has to be able to size up athletes and be able to adjust his coaching style a bit to the unique needs and character of each player, and he has to do this with the assistant coaches he leads as well. That is, he articulates a general philosophy that covers the whole team but then adjusts within that general philosophy to the particular needs of different players and assistant coaches.

Bowden is at the top of his profession, and it is not just because of his winning record. As we discussed in Chapter 6, reputations involve two broad categories of qualities. One is that you have to produce results, and Bowden has done that better than anyone. The other is that you have to do so with integrity, and he is a role model in this area. So Bobby Bowden has extensive political skill, and he employs it quite effectively in dealing with the various constituents with whom he must interact, including the players and coaches he leads, the university president and athletic director for whom he works, and the boosters, the fans, and the local and national media. He is socially astute, interpersonally influential, well positioned in his extensive network, and he always deals with people in genuine, sincere, and authentic ways, inspiring trust, confidence, and liking—a politically skilled person, indeed.

J. Dennis Hastert—now best known as Speaker of the House in the U.S. Congress—started out as a high school teacher and coach. It is those skills, competencies, and demeanor that he brings to his current leadership role, illustrating the basic truth that the skill sets and competencies of coach and politician—and corporate executive—are essentially the same.

Although politicians usually demonstrate political skill in more public and visible ways, Hastert's understated, humble demeanor has proven effective in both coaching and politics. Still referred to as "Coach" on Capitol Hill, he is the epitome of political skill—so skilled that he appears to have no political skill at all. His style comes across as genuine and sincere, just the way he is. An example of the person who becomes the role, he is truly "what-you-see-is-what-you-get" (Franzen, 2003).

Hastert seems to view self-importance as an affliction to avoid. "I'm not saying I'm a humble person," he says; "I wouldn't blow my own horn on humility" (quoted in Franzen, 2003, p. 85). Hastert shuns the public eye, preferring to let others speak to the media. His predecessor, Newt Gingrich, basked in the glow of media attention; Hastert avoids it. Neither flamboyant nor a showman, he quietly goes about his job of leading the House of Representatives.

By building networks, alliances, and coalitions, he has developed a store of social capital he can use to push through policies that reflect the strong sentiments of his party and his ideology. He is, by necessity, a power and influence broker—but he uses none of this for personal aggrandizement. It's all about service and execution of the common good and giving credit to others. In fact, Bill Lipinski, the ranking House Democrat from Illinois, said, "He isn't a boaster or a credit-grabber. . . . He's one of the nicest, friendliest, most cooperative human beings I've ever been involved with in politics" (Franzen, 2003, p. 94).

The world of Washington politics is known for manipulation of images, self-interest, spin, and sometimes questionable integrity. Whether it is really that way or not, most hold this perception. This makes a person with Hastert's qualities of honesty and authenticity a refreshing change of pace for that arena. He's a Midwestern farm boy, raised by a set of basic values he has never forgotten and that he lives by today. His reputation embodies these values and contributes to his ability to be influential. As a person of integrity, he knows how to lead by example and by facilitating and coaching people to realize the outcomes he has orchestrated for the legislature. Of course, he is no different in his current job from what he was as a high school coach.

And how is it that we seem to have such familiarity with Hastert and his political skill? Forty years ago, when Yorkville High School in Illinois hired him to teach economics and sociology and to coach wrestling and football, two of us were students there. Sherry Davidson was a junior, and Gerald Ferris a freshman who went on to play football and wrestle for Hastert for four years. We can tell you quite confidently and without qualification that J. Dennis Hastert has the rare ability to bring out the best in people, whether they are students and athletes or political leaders. That is, he simply has great political skill.

Conclusion

The skills needed to ensure leader effectiveness and subsequent group success have changed to emphasize factors such as social acuity and interpersonal astuteness, or what we call political skill. If you assume that one critical job of the leader is to eliminate barriers that might hinder team effectiveness, then some degree of political skill is essential. As we see it, Shelley Kirkpatrick and Edwin Locke sum up the situation perfectly: "It is unequivocally clear that leaders are not like other people. Leaders do not have to be great men or women by being intellectual geniuses or omniscient prophets to succeed, but they do need to have the right stuff: and this stuff is not equally present in all people" (1991, p. 58). We believe that political skill represents a big part of the "right stuff."

9

SUMMARIZING THE ESSENCE OF POLITICAL SKILL

The workplace is a social world, which is why political skill is critically important there today. Politics goes on in all organizations, though with more intensity in some than in others, and even where it is at its mildest you need political skill to be effective at getting things done. Organizational politics is commonly viewed as a negative influence, but we subscribe to the neutral view (shared by a number of scholars and practitioners) that sees politics as a necessary and pervasive feature of organizational life. Therefore, given that political skill is what allows people to navigate the sometimes turbulent organizational waters, we regard it as a positive quality that can contribute to successful careers and impressive personal and professional reputations.

Of course, just like any other quality or characteristic intended for positive use, political skill can be used in a purely self-interested way that hurts others and organizations. Some politically skilled corporate executives have used this competency to make themselves richer at the expense of many other employees and shareholders, and their organizations overall, as at Enron, Tyco, and WorldCom. That kind of behavior represents a misuse of the tool, however, not a flaw in the tool itself.

Political Skill in Practice

What can political skill do for you? This is the overriding question of the book, and much goes into the answer. To recap briefly, what we have covered in this book comes down to four main areas. We have discussed

- The nature of political skill

- How to measure it

- How it can be developed

- What roles it can play in your success in the workplace

Our conclusions in each of these areas, summarized here, result from more than fifteen years of studying this fascinating topic. Our work has included a great deal of research, enhanced by use of the *Political Skill Inventory* we developed (which is introduced in Chapter 2 and further discussed in the Appendix).

Nature of Political Skill

Political skill shows itself in four dimensions: social astuteness, interpersonal influence, networking ability, and apparent sincerity. These four, which provide the main themes of the book, are discussed liberally throughout the book—in relation to the measurement and development of political skill in Part One and again in each of the specific roles featured in the chapters in Part Two.

Measuring Political Skill

By answering the eighteen questions in the *Political Skill Inventory* in Chapter 2, you can measure how much general political skill you possess. You can also come away with an understanding of how much political skill you have in each of the four political skill dimensions. The inventory is easy to take and administer, whether you are curious about your own political skill level or that of someone else.

Developing Political Skill

How do some individuals identified as high in political skill approach the practice of their craft? Research supports the finding that drama-based training, executive coaching, and mentoring appear to be the most common, as well as most effective, methods for developing political skill in all its aspects. Other training techniques and methods specific to one or another of the four dimensions include critique and feedback sessions, videotaped role-playing with feedback, leadership training, and behavioral modeling.

Another interesting area of related research shows that women and minorities are deficient in political skill when compared to their male mainstream counterparts in the workplace. As more women and minorities find their way into higher levels of organizations, these findings may change.

Roles of Political Skill

Political skill plays a role in everything you do from the minute you embark on your career. Of course, it is also an integral part of your personal and social life, but for the purpose of this book, we have focused on political skill in the workplace. Consequently, we have highlighted how it affects your ability to get hired; your job performance and career success wherever your career path leads you, in one organization or several; the enhancement of your reputation; your way of managing job stress; and your approach to building your leadership potential and that of your team.

Conclusion

The very essence of political skill is to be influential in such a way that you do not appear to be trying to exert influence. Therefore, the true mark of a politically skilled person is to appear *not* to have political skill—but instead, to come across as a genuine, sincere, authentic person. Those high in political skill have a calm, self-assured, personally secure manner and bearing that draws people to them, which also enhances their ability to be influential.

Some may characterize politically skilled individuals as chameleon-like in their ability to adapt to different and changing situations. This analogy can be quite useful; however, unlike cold-blooded chameleons, politically skilled people can demonstrate functional adaptability and flexibility even when the situational cues for what type of behavior is required are unclear. A plaid background can present a dilemma for a chameleon, but the politically skilled person quickly and effortlessly sizes up a similarly complex social situation and almost instinctively knows just what to do. This is the essence of political skill.

APPENDIX

RELATIONSHIP OF POLITICAL SKILL TO OTHER CONCEPTS: RESEARCH RESULTS

The *Political Skill Inventory* presented in Chapter 2 has been subjected to extensive research and validation. Here we discuss the rationale and findings reported in "Development and Validation of the Political Skill Inventory" (Ferris et al., 2005).

In our view, political skill is not simply synonymous with influence tactics, and it is not related to assertiveness—political skill is a style. It is positively correlated with self-monitoring (the extent to which you are aware of your environment and responsive to interpersonal cues) and conscientiousness (the extent to which you are attentive to deadlines and finding the best solutions to problems at work). In addition, we believe that political skill is inversely related to general anxiety, meaning that politically skilled individuals are apt to experience less stress and strain than their less skillful counterparts.

We have examined three types of influence tactics: coalition forming, upward appeal, and assertiveness. Coalition forming involves trying to gain support from others by getting them to buy into an idea. Upward appeals are attempts to gain influence by appealing for support from higher-ups. Assertiveness means being forthright with requests and information. These influence tactics are by no means certain to work every time; their success depends largely on their suitability for the circumstances and on how they are implemented.

Preliminary results provide evidence for the validity of the political skill construct. As expected, the overall political skill construct was significantly and positively related to self-monitoring ($r = .39$, $p < .001$) and conscientiousness ($r = .31$, $p < .001$). The social astuteness dimension of political skill demonstrated the strongest correlation of the four dimensions with both self-monitoring ($r = .37$, $p < .001$) and conscientiousness ($r = .27$, $p < .001$). However, the differences among the correlations for these two constructs with the other three PSI dimensions were not statistically significant.

Results also showed evidence that political skill is not redundant with influence tactics. Indeed, none of the correlations between political skill and the individual influence tactics was extremely high. Specifically, political skill was related to upward appeal ($r = .25$, $p < .001$) and coalition forming ($r = .21$, $p < .001$). Our expectation that political skill, being more indirect, would not correlate highly with assertiveness was borne out; the correlation ($r = .09$, *n.s.*) was not significant.

Because the nature of networking implies involvement with others and being able to mobilize coalitions for influence, networking ability was hypothesized to demonstrate the strongest positive relationship with the upward appeal and coalition forming influence tactics, and that was found to be the case ($r = .30$, $p < .001$; $r = .31$, $p < .001$, respectively). The networking ability dimension was thought to provide the positioning to allow one to employ assertiveness effectively. Indeed, networking ability demonstrated a significant positive correlation with assertiveness ($r = .18$, $p < .001$), a greater correlation than the correlations of any of the other PSI dimensions.

Political skill exhibited a significant negative correlation with trait anxiety ($r = -.31$, $p < .001$). We expected the feelings of control and personal security that result from scoring high on the interpersonal influence dimension of political skill to be associated with reduced anxiety, and results supported this: interpersonal influence reflected the largest negative correlation with trait anxiety of any of the four dimensions ($r = -.37$, $p < .001$). Furthermore, when conducting significance tests between correlations of interpersonal influence and trait anxiety with each other PSI dimension and trait anxiety, all correlations were significantly smaller in magnitude.

In another study, we again expected political skill to be positively correlated with self-monitoring and with conscientiousness. The overall PSI did positively correlate with self-monitoring ($r = .33$, $p < .01$). Interestingly, though positive, the correlation of the PSI with conscientiousness was not significant in this study. Furthermore, our work confirmed the prediction of Chao, O'Leary-Kelly, Wolf, Klein, and Gardner (1994) that political skill should be positively correlated with political savvy, with the overall PSI correlating significantly with political savvy ($r = .47$, $p < .001$).

Social astuteness demonstrated the highest correlation with self-monitoring ($r = .32$, $p < .001$) and with political savvy ($r = .60$, $p < .001$) of any of the four political skill dimensions. Political skill should be related to various influence tactics, including upward appeal and coalition tactics, but not to assertiveness, as was found in the first study. Results provided evidence that political skill is not redundant with influence tactics. The PSI total score positively correlated with the coalition tactic ($r = .28$, $p < .01$), and it did not correlate with assertiveness ($r = .16$, $n.s.$). However, the PSI exhibited a positive, though not significant, correlation with the upward appeal tactic.

The networking ability dimension was positively related to the upward appeal influence tactic ($r = .26$, $p < .05$), the coalition tactic ($r = .30$, $p < .01$), and the assertiveness tactic ($r = .22$, $p < .05$). Additionally, political skill should be negatively related to trait anxiety such that politically skilled individuals are apt to experience less anxiety or tension. Results show that the PSI indeed was inversely related to trait anxiety ($r = -.27$, $p < .01$), as found in the first study. Also replicating results from the first study, interpersonal influence showed the strongest relationship with trait anxiety ($r = -.42$, $p < .01$), and correlations of trait anxiety with all other PSI dimensions were found to be significantly smaller in magnitude.

Overall, these studies give strong support for the validity of political skill. In other words, these studies demonstrate that our questionnaire designed to measure political skill is, in fact, measuring political skill and not some other concept. Essentially, this research provides strong support that our questionnaire is measuring what it is supposed to measure.

References

Ahearn, K. K., Ferris, G. R., Hochwarter, W. A., Douglas, C., & Ammeter, A. P. (2004). Leader political skill and team performance. *Journal of Management, 30,* 309–327.

As leaders, women rule. (2000, November 20). *BusinessWeek,* p. 74.

Bandura, A. (1986). *Social foundations of thought and action: A social cognitive theory.* Englewood Cliffs, NJ: Prentice-Hall.

Baron, R. A., & Markman, G. D. (2000). Beyond social capital: How social skills can enhance entrepreneurs' success. *Academy of Management Executive, 14,* 106–116.

Bartol, K. M., & Martin, D. C. (1990). When politics pays: Factors influencing managerial compensation decisions. *Personnel Psychology, 43,* 599–614.

Batt, R., & Appelbaum, E. (1995). Worker participation in diverse settings: Does the form affect the outcome, and if so, who benefits? *British Journal of Industrial Relations, 33,* 353–378.

Bell, E. L. J., & Nkomo, S. M. (2001). *Our separate ways: Black and white women and the struggle for professional identity.* Boston: Harvard Business School Press.

Block, J., & Kremen, A. (1996). IQ and ego-resiliency: Conceptual and empirical connections and separateness. *Journal of Personality and Social Psychology, 70,* 349–361.

Bolino, M. C. (1999). Citizenship and impression management: Good soldiers or good actors? *Academy of Management Review, 24,* 82–98.

Bolman, L. G., & Deal, T. E. (1991). *Reframing organizations: Artistry, choice, and leadership.* San Francisco: Jossey-Bass.

Borman, W. C., Hedge, J. W., Ferstl, K. L., Kaufman, J. D., Farmer, W. L., & Bearden, R. M. (2003). Current directions and issues in personnel selection and classification. In J. J. Martocchio & G. R. Ferris (Eds.), *Research in personnel and human resources management* (Vol. 22, pp. 287–355). Oxford, England: JAI Press/Elsevier Science.

Borman, W. C., & Motowidlo, S. J. (1993). Expanding the criterion domain to include elements of contextual performance. In N. Schmitt & W. C. Borman (Eds.), *Personnel selection* (pp. 71–98). San Francisco: Jossey-Bass.

Bowden, B. (2001). *The Bowden way: 50 years of leadership wisdom.* Atlanta: Longstreet Press.

Buckman, R. H. (2004). *Building a knowledge-driven organization.* New York: McGraw-Hill.

Byrne, J. A. (1999). *Chainsaw: The notorious career of Al Dunlap.* New York: HarperCollins.

Campbell, J. P. (1990). Modeling the performance prediction problem in industrial and organizational psychology. In M. D. Dunnette & L. M. Hough (Eds.), *Handbook of industrial and organizational psychology* (2nd ed., Vol. 1, pp. 687–732). Mountain View, CA: Davies-Black Publishing.

Carnegie, D. (1936). *How to win friends and influence people.* New York: Simon & Schuster.

Cascio, W. F. (1995). Whither industrial and organizational psychology in a changing world of work? *American Psychologist, 50,* 928–939.

Chao, G. T., O'Leary-Kelly, A. M., Wolf, S., Klein, H. J., & Gardner, P. D. (1994). Organizational socialization: Its content and consequences. *Journal of Applied Psychology, 79,* 730–743.

Clinton, B, (2004). *My life.* New York: Knopf.

The Clinton legacy. (2001, January 14). *Tallahassee Democrat,* pp. 1A, 6A.

Cooper, W. H., Graham, W. J., & Dyke, L. S. (1993). Tournament players. In G. R. Ferris (Ed.), *Research in personnel and human resources management* (Vol. 11, pp. 83–132). Greenwich, CT: JAI Press.

Cotterell, B. (2002, December 19). Political skills important for job. *Tallahassee Democrat,* pp. 1A, 4A.

Daft, R. L., & Lewin, A. Y. (1993). Where are the theories for the "new" organizational forms? An editorial essay. *Organization Science, 4,* i-iv.

Dauten, D. (1996, July 8). Promote yourself using the art of 'schmoozilitics.' *Chicago Tribune,* Section 4, p. 2.

Dess, G. G., & Shaw, J. D. (2001). Voluntary turnover, social capital, and organizational performance. *Academy of Management Review, 26,* 446–456.

Deutsch, C. H. (1990, January 21). Media manipulation 101. *New York Times,* p. F29.

Drake, G. (1987, February 10). Acting classes for the political world. *New York Times*, p. 22.

Dulebohn, J. H., Ferris, G. R., & Stodd, J. T. (1995). The history and evolution of human resource management. In G. R. Ferris, S. D. Rosen, & D. T. Barnum (Eds.), *Handbook of human resource management* (pp. 18–41). Oxford, England: Blackwell.

Edelman, M. (1964). *The symbolic uses of politics*. Urbana, IL: University of Illinois Press.

Fernandez, J. P. (1981). *Racism and sexism in corporate life*. Lexington, MA: Lexington Books.

Ferris, G. R., Judge, T. A., Rowland, K. M., & Fitzgibbons, D. E. (1994). Subordinate influence and the performance evaluation process: Test of a model. *Organizational Behavior and Human Decision Processes, 58,* 101–135.

Ferris, G. R., Treadway, D. C., Kolodinsky, R. W., Hochwarter, W. A., Kacmar, C. J., Douglas, C., & Frink, D. D. (2005). Development and validation of the political skill inventory. *Journal of Management, 31,* 126–152.

Fombrun, C. J. (1996). *Reputation: Realizing value from corporate image*. Boston: Harvard Business School Press.

Franzen, J. (2003, October 6). The listener. *New Yorker,* pp. 85–99.

Frink, D. D., & Ferris, G. R. (1998). Accountability, impression management, and goal setting in the performance evaluation process. *Human Relations, 51,* 1259–1283.

Gardner, H. (1995). *Leading minds: An anatomy of leadership*. New York: Basic Books.

Gardner, W. L., & Avolio, B. J. (1998). The charismatic relationship: A dramaturgical perspective. *Academy of Management Review, 23,* 32–58.

Garson, H. S. (2004). *Oprah Winfrey: A biography*. Westport, CT: Greenwood Press.

Gilmore, D. C., & Ferris, G. R. (1989). The effects of applicant impression management tactics on interviewer judgments. *Journal of Management, 15,* 557–564.

Gilmore, D. C., Stevens, C. K., Harrell-Cook, G., & Ferris, G. R. (1999). Impression management tactics. In R. W. Eder & M. M. Harris (Eds.), *The employment interview handbook* (pp. 321–336). Thousand Oaks, CA: Sage.

Giuliani, R. (2002). *Leadership*. New York: Miramax Books.

Goffman, E. (1959). *The presentation of self in everyday life*. Garden City, NY: Doubleday.

Goleman, D. (1995). *Emotional intelligence*. New York: Bantam Books.

Goleman, D. (1998). *Working with emotional intelligence*. New York: Bantam Books.

Gould, S., & Penley, L. E. (1984). Career strategies and salary progression: A study of their relationship in a municipal bureaucracy. *Organizational Behavior and Human Performance, 34,* 244–265.

Graen, G. B., & Uhl-Bien, M. (1995). Relationship-based approach to leadership: Development of leader-member exchange (LMX) theory of leadership over 25 years: Applying a multi-level multi-domain perspective. *Leadership Quarterly, 6,* 219–247.

Greenstein, F. I. (2004). *The presidential difference: Leadership style from FDR to George W. Bush.* Princeton, NJ: Princeton University Press.

Higgins, C. A. (2000). *The effect of applicant influence tactics on recruiter perceptions of fit.* Unpublished doctoral dissertation, Department of Management and Organizations, University of Iowa.

Hochschild, A. R. (1983). *The managed heart: Commercialization of human feeling.* Berkeley: University of California Press.

House, R. J., & Aditya, R. N. (1997). The social scientific study of leadership: Quo vadis? *Journal of Management, 23,* 409–473.

Isaacson, K. (2004). Getting hired. *Women in Business, 56,* 14—17.

Jackall, R. (1988). *Moral mazes: The world of corporate managers.* New York: Oxford University Press.

Job security: Collect those brownie points. (1996, March 4). *Chicago Tribune,* Section 4, p. 3.

Judge, T. A., Colbert, A. E., & Ilies, R. (2004). Intelligence and leadership: A quantitative review and test of theoretical propositions. *Journal of Applied Psychology, 89,* 542–552.

Kanter, D. L., & Mirvis, P. H. (1989). *The cynical Americans: Living and working in an age of discontent and disillusion.* San Francisco: Jossey-Bass.

Kanter, R. M. (2004). *Confidence: How winning streaks and losing streaks begin and end.* New York: Crown Business.

Kelley, R. & Kaplan, J. (1993). How Bell Labs creates star performers. *Harvard Business Review, 71,* 128–136.

Khurana, R. (2002). *Searching for a corporate savior: The irrational quest for charismatic CEOs.* Princeton, NJ: Princeton University Press.

Kipnis, D., & Schmidt, S. M. (1988). Upward influence styles: Relationships with performance evaluations, salary, and stress. *Administrative Science Quarterly, 33,* 528–542.

Kirkpatrick, S. A., & Locke, E. A. (1991). Leadership: Do traits matter? *Academy of Management Executive, 5,* 48–60.

Klaus, P. (2003). *Brag! The art of tooting your own horn without blowing it.* New York: Warner Books.

Leary, M. R. (1995). *Self-presentation: Impression management and interpersonal behavior.* Boulder, CO: Westview Press.

Logan, D. A. (2001). Libel law in the trenches: Reflections on current data on libel litigation. *Virginia Law Review, 87,* 503–529.

Lombardo, M., & McCauley, C. (1988). *The dynamics of management derailment.* Technical report #34. Greensboro, NC: Center for Creative Leadership.

Luthans, F., Hodgetts, R. M., & Rosenkrantz, S. A. (1988). *Real managers.* Cambridge, MA: Ballinger.

Mainiero, L. A. (1994). On breaking the glass ceiling: The political seasoning of powerful women executives. *Organizational Dynamics, 22,* 5–20.

Mann, S. (1995). Politics and power in organizations: Why women lose out. *Leadership & Organization Development Journal, 16*(2), 9–15.

Marchica, J. (2004). *The accountable organization.* Mountain View, CA: Davies-Black Publishing.

Matthews, C. (1988). *Hardball: How politics is played told by one who knows the game.* New York: HarperCollins.

Mintzberg, H. (1983). *Power in and around organizations.* Englewood Cliffs, NJ: Prentice-Hall.

Morrow, L. (1998, March 30). The trouble with the present tense. *Time,* p. 29.

Mount, M. K., & Barrick, M. R. (1995). The Big Five personality dimensions: Implications for research and practice in human resources management. In G. R. Ferris (Ed.), *Research in personnel and human resources management* (Vol. 13, pp. 153–200). Greenwich, CT: JAI Press.

Münsterberg, H. (1913). *Psychology and industrial efficiency.* Boston: Houghton Mifflin.

Murphy, K. R., & Cleveland, J. N. (1995). *Understanding performance appraisal: Social, organizational, and goal-based perspectives.* Thousand Oaks, CA: Sage.

Perrewé, P. L., Zellars, K. L., Ferris, G. R., Rossi, A. M., Kacmar, C. J., & Ralston, D. A. (2004). Neutralizing job stressors: Political skill as an antidote to the dysfunctional consequences of role conflict stressors. *Academy of Management Journal, 47,* 141–152.

Peters, T. (1987). *Thriving on chaos: Handbook for a management revolution.* New York: Knopf.

Pfeffer, J. (1981). *Power in organizations.* Boston: Pitman.

Pfeffer, J. (1992). *Managing with power: Politics and influence in organizations.* Boston: Harvard Business School Press.

Pondy, L. R. (1978). Leadership as a language game. In M. W. McCall & M. M. Lombardo (Eds.), *Leadership: Where else can we go?* (pp. 87–99). Durham, NC: Duke University Press.

Purnick, J. (2004, September 13). Testing clout of Giuliani in the G.O.P. *New York Times,* Section B, p. 1.

Rosen, B., & Lovelace, K. (1991). Piecing together the diversity puzzle. *HR Magazine, 36,* 78–84.

Russ, G. S. (1991). Symbolic communication and image management in organizations. In R. A. Giacalone & P. Rosenfeld (Eds.), *Applied impression management: How image-making affects managerial decisions* (pp. 219–240). Newbury Park, CA: Sage.

Schmidt, F. L., & Hunter, J. E. (1998). The validity and utility of selection methods in personnel psychology: Practical and theoretical implications of 85 years of research findings. *Psychological Bulletin, 124,* 262–274.

Seibert, S. E., Kraimer, M. L., & Liden, R. C. (2001). A social capital theory of career success. *Academy of Management Journal, 44,* 219–237.

Semadar, A. (2004). *Interpersonal competencies and managerial performance: The role of emotional intelligence, leadership self-efficacy, self-monitoring, and political skill.* Unpublished doctoral dissertation, Department of Psychology, University of Melbourne, Australia.

Sofer, C. (1970). *Men in mid-career: A study of British managers and technical specialities.* Cambridge, England: Cambridge University Press.

Spence, A. M. (1974). *Market signaling: Informational transfer in hiring and related screening processes.* Cambridge, MA: Harvard University Press.

St. George, J., Schwager, S., & Canavan, F. (2000, Autumn). A guide to drama-based training. *National Productivity Review,* pp. 15–19.

Staw, B., & Barsade, S. G. (1993). Affect and managerial performance: A test of the sadder-but-wiser vs. happier-and-smarter hypothesis. *Administrative Science Quarterly, 38,* 304–331.

Staw, B., Sutton, R., & Pelled, L. (1994). Employee positive emotions and favorable outcomes at the workplace. *Organization Science, 5,* 51–71.

Stengel, R. (2000). *You're too kind: A brief history of flattery.* New York: Simon & Schuster.

Suchman, M. C. (1995). Managing legitimacy: Strategic and institutional approaches. *Academy of Management Review, 20,* 571–610.

Thomas, L. & Ganster, D. (1995). Impact of family-supportive work variables on work-family conflict and strain: A control perspective. *Journal of Applied Psychology, 80,* 6–15.

Thorndike, E. L. (1920). Intelligence and its uses. *Harper's, 140,* 227–235.

Towler, A., & Dipboye, R. L. (2001). *Effects of charismatic communication training on motivation, behavior, and attitudes.* Paper presented at the 16th Annual Conference of the Society for Industrial and Organizational Psychology, San Diego.

Treadway, D. C., Ferris, G. R., Douglas, C., Hochwarter, W. A., Kacmar, C. J., Ammeter, A. P., & Buckley, M. R. (2004). Leader political skill and employee reactions. *Leadership Quarterly, 15,* 493–513.

Up and out: Rude awakenings come early. *Chicago Tribune* (1995, November 10), Section 4, p. 3.

Watkins, M. D., & Bazerman, M. H. (2003, March). Predictable surprises: The disasters you should have seen coming. *Harvard Business Review*, pp. 72–80.

Weick, K. E. (1979). Cognitive processes in organizations. In B. M. Staw (Ed.), *Research in organizational behavior* (Vol. 1, pp. 41–74). Greenwich, CT: JAI Press.

Worker stress, health reaching critical point. (1999, May). *American Psychological Association Monitor*, pp. 1, 27.

Wright, J. P. (1979). *On a clear day you can see General Motors.* New York: Avon Books.

INDEX